OVER FLOW

A DAILY EXPERIENCE
OF HEAVEN'S ABUNDANCE

Rom 11:6
GRACE NO
MORE GRACE

Chris & Liz Gore

Overflow
Copyright © 2016—Chris and Liz Gore
Second Print

All rights reserved. This book is protected by the copyright laws of the United States of America. This book may not be copied or reprinted for commercial gain or profit. The use of short quotations or occasional page copying for personal or group study is permitted and encouraged. Permission will be granted upon request.

Unless otherwise identified, Scripture quotations are taken from the NKJV the New King James Version. Copyright © 1982 by Thomas Nelson, Inc. Used by permission. All rights reserved.

Cover by Amy Miller | www.amymiller.design
Interior by Renee Evans | www.reneeevansdesign.com

www.facebook.com/chrissgore
www.instagram.com/chrissgore
Website: www.kingdomreleasers.org
Email: overflow@kingdomreleasers.org
ISBN: 978-0-9905752-8-3

Printed in the United States

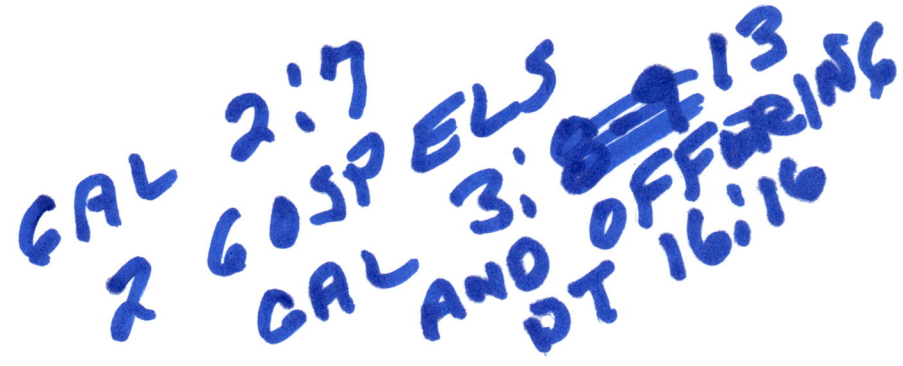

GAL 2:7
2 GOSPELS =13
GAL 3:
GAL AND OFFERING
DT 16:16

DEDICATION

This book is dedicated to our 3 incredible daughters. Charlotte, Emma and Sophie. We decided early in parenthood that we would live sacrificially if it meant our children would thrive in life. We have decided that all the profit from this book would be passed to them so they can receive the education they desire, without having to accumulate student debt.

Charlotte, Emma and Sophie, while you each have extremely different giftings, personalities, and callings, we are so proud of each of you young ladies, you are truly the delight of our hearts.

We also wish to thank Angie Wenstrom, personal assistant to Chris, for the countless hours you poured into helping make this project come together. We are so incredibly thankful for you and the way that you continue to shine in all that life brings your way!

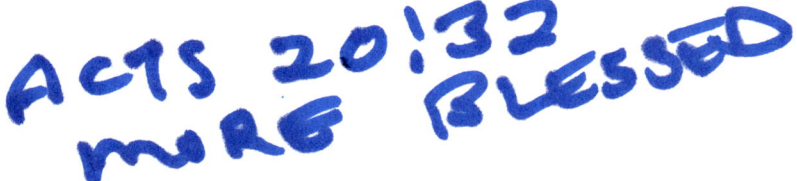

ACTS 20:32
MORE BLESSED

GAL 2:19
1 COR 15:3-8-12
f GAL AND OFFERING
DT 16:16

ACTS 20:32
MAY BLESSED

INTRODUCTION

As a healing minister, I get to meet thousands of people from all different cultures and countries. I have discovered that while cultures vary greatly, one thing that does not are the daily pressures people face.

My heart for many years has been to see people healed and to be activated to heal the sick. But even more than my heart to see people healed, I want to see them walk in wholeness in every part of their lives: spiritually, physically, and emotionally.

It is when we are whole spiritually, physically, and emotionally that we are enabled to walk in longevity. One of my greatest areas of concern is that people do not know how to walk strong spiritually. Jesus said He is coming back for a victorious bride. I want to see strong people, people that know how to spiritually feed themselves, walk in the fullness of the abundant life of which Jesus speaks.

I wrote this book because I see so many people's lives built on lies and a misunderstanding of the heart of the Father.

OVERFLOW

Overflow is intended to be practical and filled with stories to bring encouragement, while offering some "nuggets" of food to feed on so we can learn to operate in the overflow of Heaven.

May God's grace increase in every area of your life, as you feast on the goodness of a loving Father.

Stay thirsty my friends,

Chris Gore

TAKING CARE OF OUR FOUNDATIONS

TODAY'S SCRIPTURE

And to the angel of the church in Sardis write, "'These things says He who has the seven Spirits of God and the seven stars: 'I know your works, that you have a name that you are alive, but you are dead. Be watchful, and strengthen the things which remain, that are ready to die, for I have not found your works perfect before God. Remember therefore how you have received and heard; hold fast and repent. Therefore if you will not watch, I will come upon you as a thief, and you will not know what hour I will come upon you.'"

REVELATION 3:1-3

I have been pondering the past six months on a subject that is not new to any of us: the importance of taking care of our foundations, both in our character and spiritual life. It's easy to get so busy that we stop taking care of the foundational things in our lives, and cracks slowly begin to form.

There is a story in history about the city of Sardis, which is one of the seven churches in Revelation. Sardis was located high on top of sheer cliffs that were almost impossible to climb. Because of its location, the people thought their city was impenetrable. They felt that foreign aggressors could not make war on them and they became proud, cocky, over-confident, lazy and complacent.

As a result of their haughty attitude, they stopped taking care of the foundation and walls. While their pride and over-confidence grew, they failed to notice the walls had begun to crack and deteriorate. Larger cracks began to form at the base of the walls.

At first, the cracks were small and not noticeable, but as time moved on, those tiny cracks grew deeper and wider. Finally, the gaps in the walls became so wide that a human could easily slip through them. Meanwhile the town failed to notice they were no longer secure.

One night while the city of Sardis was sleeping, an enemy scaled the cliff and went through the cracks. The city of Sardis was easily occupied by the enemy without any resistance.

I don't tell this story to create fear or to correct anyone, but to bring to our attention that while in the midst of the most amazing breakthroughs we have ever seen, (which are not necessarily a measure of our relationship with God), neglecting to care for the small cracks, both in our character and spiritual lives, can result in large cracks in our foundation and ultimately losing our sensitivity to the Spirit of God.

When I took my car in for service several months back, I was advised that there were leaks in the radiator that needed attention. In my busyness of life, the cracks were not addressed and ultimately 8 months later the leaks blew up my car engine, costing me thousands of dollars. This could have been easily prevented if I had taken the time to fix the small cracks beforehand.

PERSONAL APPLICATION

1. Based off the story, what is the foundation that I build my life on?

2. At this time in my life, how successful do I feel I am at managing my foundation?

OVERFLOW

3. What does it look like on a practical and daily basis to guard my foundation against cracks that the enemy could penetrate?

4. What action steps could I take to become more aware of guarding my foundation against cracks?

DECLARE THIS TODAY

I declare by faith that I am sensitive to the Spirit of God! The Holy Spirit shows me every area of my life that is weak and needs attention. When the Holy Spirit speaks to me, I am quick to listen and quick to obey. I urgently act to bring correction to every weakness in my character and my spiritual life where the enemy might try to penetrate. Therefore, the enemy has no access to me!

WATCH OVER YOURSELF

TODAY'S SCRIPTURE

Therefore let him who thinks he stands take heed lest he fall.

CORINTHIANS 10:12

The apostle Paul gave us a warning us in 1 Corinthians 10:12. The two words "thinks" and "stands," or in the King James "thinketh" and "standeth," come from two Greek words: *dokeō*[1] which means, "to suppose, to think, to reckon, or to be of the opinion" and *histēmi*[2] which means, "to stand, to stand firm, or to stand upright."

However, when we put these two Greek words together in a phrase as the Apostle Paul used them here, the first half of the verse could actually read, "Therefore, let anyone who has a self-imposed opinion of himself, that he is standing strong and firm…"

---

[1] 2010. Strong's #1380: *dokeō* - Greek/Hebrew Definitions - Bible Tools.

[2] 2015. Strong's G2476 - *histēmi* - Blue Letter Bible - Lexicon.

When the Apostle Paul goes on to say, "take heed lest he fall," the word "fall" in Greek is the word *piptō*[3] which means, "to fall, or to fall into a worse state than before." It can also mean, "someone that falls into some kind of failure, or falls into ruin."

The word the Apostle Paul uses here actually describes a downfall from a formerly presumed high and haughty position. So it's not merely a stumble, it is a downward plummet that leads to a sorrowful crash.

If we restructure this verse how I believe the Apostle Paul meant it to read, then it could perhaps be read like this: "If anyone has the opinion of himself that he is standing strong and firm, he needs to be continually watchful and always on his guard lest he trip, stumble, or fall from his over-confident position and take a nose-dive into a serious crash."

In the previous devotional, "Taking Care of Our Foundations," we saw the church in Sardis had the same mindset as the rest of the city of Sardis. Jesus told them in Revelation 3:1, "I know your works, that you have a name that you are alive, but you are dead."

I have found over the years of maturing in my own walk with the Lord, that as I grow in confidence of who I am in Him and who He is in me, I must still guard against falling into complacency. We can do the works of the Lord and see the most powerful miracles all around us, but we must remember those miracles are not a measuring stick of our relationship with God. It's so important that we continue to

---

[3] "Hebrew - Greek Key Word Study Bible - NASB - Parable Christian Stores." 2011. 18 Jul. 2016

be watchful and strengthen the areas in our lives which need attention, so cracks don't become gaping holes.

Jesus goes on to say in Revelation 3:2, "Be watchful and strengthen the things which remain, that you are ready to die, for I have not found your works perfect before God." I love the Gospel because Jesus always has a heart for restoration. If there is any part of us that is broken, splintered, or cracked, there is always a way for restoration. We may at times need some emergency care, but we can always be brought back to life. I prefer preventative care and fixing things along the way by remaining watchful, rather than a corrective surgery.

I challenge you today to diligently watch over your life and take care of any cracks that appear early on, so you don't need corrective surgery.

PERSONAL APPLICATION

1. Ask Jesus: Is there one or more area's of potential weakness that you want me to guard against?

OVERFLOW

2. Look back and remember an area of your life that was broken, but by God's grace was repaired and healed.

PRAY THIS TODAY

Lord, please help me to always remain diligent and watchful over my spiritual life. I recognize that I can get so busy and can wrongfully presume that I am strong. Please help me to never be smug, haughty, arrogant, or over-confident in myself, but full of the confidence of the cross instead. I pray that you would highlight the areas of my life where cracks have appeared so that I can get restored. Make me even more sensitive to you, Holy Spirit, and show me every area of my life that needs attention. As you speak I will listen and obey.

STAYING FULL

TODAY'S SCRIPTURE

And suddenly there came a sound from heaven, as of a rushing mighty wind, and it filled the whole house where they were sitting....And they were all filled with the Holy Spirit.

ACTS 2:2,4

One afternoon I was outside backwashing the pool filter. By mistake I forgot to put the filter back into normal mode. When the filter turned on at 10:00pm that night, the pool started to pump water out of the pool. In six short hours I pumped 25,000 gallons of water onto my neighbor's lawn!

I woke up the next morning, looked out my window, and in shock saw a half-filled pool. Trying to work out what went wrong, I heard the Lord speak to me and say, "Your life is just like the pool." I was confused at first and questioned what He meant. While I was outside looking at my grave error, I sensed the Lord say, "Outflow without inflow will cause you to burn out."

OVERFLOW

My pool is designed to be full. When it is full, it operates best. The manufacturing structure of my pool is designed to be filled because the water holds the sides up. If the pool remains empty, the sides will eventually implode. Without water in the pool, the filter would still turn on, but would have nothing flowing through it, and it would quickly burn out. If my pool is half-empty or completely empty, it will begin to have major issues, but those issues won't occur if my pool stays full.

My swimming pool has an auto-fill setting on it. As the sun evaporates the water, the auto-fill keeps it topped up. I accidentally had forgotten to turn the auto-fill back on that night, but even if it was on, the outflow would have still been faster than the inflow, eventually causing my filter to burn out.

Friends, we can only give away what we take in, yet many of us try to give away more than what they are take in. This might work for a season, but eventually it will cause our lives to implode and burn out.

In Scripture we see that God rarely appears in a hurry. There are only a few references in which we see Heaven rush. One of these instances is the story of the prayer meeting in the Upper Room in Acts 1 and 2.

"When the Day of Pentecost had fully come, they were all with one accord in one place. And suddenly there came a sound from heaven, as of a rushing mighty wind, and it filled the whole house where they were sitting" (Acts 2:1-2).

Jesus actually wants to fill us daily with His presence! When we position ourselves to receive, Heaven is actually in a hurry to fill and refresh us. It's not fun to give from our limited reserves, but giving away Jesus out of the abundance of our overflow is easy.

If you want longevity in your life, make sure you have your auto-fill turned on and you are getting filled afresh by Jesus on a daily basis.

PERSONAL APPLICATION

1. Am I taking time daily to allow Heaven to come and fill my life?

2. What steps can I take to make sure that my inflow stays greater than my outflow?

OVERFLOW

3. How can I more effectively position myself to receive the infilling from Heaven?

4. How can I restructure my life so that my auto-fill can stay turned on?

PRAY THIS TODAY

Father, I thank you that it is Heaven's desire that I remain full. I thank you that I am a vessel capable of receiving. I choose to reactivate my auto-fill button to allow Heaven to not only fill me, but to fill me to overflowing so that I will have more to give away to the world around me. I choose now to receive from you as a good Father and I believe that when I, as your child, ask you for bread that you do not give a stone in return. Thank you for the gift of the Holy Spirit.

NOTHING IS SMALL IN THE KINGDOM

by *CLEMENT SIM*
Intern to Chris Gore 2016

TODAY'S SCRIPTURE

For who has despised the day of small things?
ZECHARIAH 4:10

When I first found out that I was accepted to Bethel School of Supernatural Ministry (BSSM), I was really excited for the new season. However, once I found out how much money I was going to need, I started to panic and fear the worst. I estimated a budget of about $15,000 and I was starting with $0. However, God spoke to me and asked me to start sharing about my new journey with my friends. In the beginning, some friends came forward and blessed me with $50. Instead of being thankful, I viewed the amount as small compared to my almost impossible goal. I was not excited about the small seed initially.

In such moments, we can choose to be ungrateful or we can choose to give thanks, even if it's a small beginning. As

I began to give thanks, more people began to give. It started to increase to a $100 gift, then a $500 gift, and then $2,000 by a generous friend! Here is a thought. If we cannot celebrate the $50 we receive, what makes us think we can celebrate the $2,000 when we receive it? There is nothing too small to be thankful for in our lives. It can be as simple as the bed we get to sleep in, the food we get to eat, or even the sun we get to enjoy.

Nothing in the Kingdom is insignificant. Here are two examples from the Bible. In Matthew 13, Jesus said the mustard seed was the smallest seed, yet it was able to become a large tree that the birds could nest in. Even though we cannot see the tree from the seed, the DNA and potential of the tree is inside the seed. I'd like to suggest that some of the breakthroughs in our life will come in the form of a mustard seed. If we focus on how small the seed is and do nothing with it, nothing will happen. But if we steward that small seed with thanksgiving, not despising how insignificant it might appear, it can grow into a huge tree.

Think for a moment about the small lunch of the little boy among the multitudes. Jesus was not bothered by the small amount of five loaves and two fishes that the boy had. Let's look at what Jesus did when He was given the small amount of food in John 6. He took the food, looked to Heaven, give thanks and broke it. I believed when He looked to Heaven, He connected with how good and how big His Father was. From that revelation, He gave thanks and believed for the increase. The small beginning resulted in overflowing multiplication of food that ended with significant leftovers.

Nothing is too insignificant for us to be thankful for and no problem is too difficult for our Father, who is the Creator of the universe. Thanksgiving increases the Kingdom in our life.

I encourage you to focus on how good our Father in Heaven is and how much bigger He is than all of your needs. Celebrate what you have in seed form and expect God to come through for you.

PERSONAL APPLICATION

1. What are some things that I can be thankful for today?

2. What are the small beginnings of breakthroughs in my life that God can multiply and increase?

OVERFLOW

3. Do I take time to focus on how big and how good my Father in Heaven is?

4. How can I daily live a lifestyle of thanksgiving daily?

> **PRAY THIS TODAY**
>
> Father, I thank you for every small beginning in my life. I believe every small seed in my life is coming to fruitfulness. I believe the seeds will have overflowing leftovers, just like the five loaves and two fish. I believe that you are for me and I know my breakthroughs are coming. I choose to give thanks for every good thing that has already happened and for every good thing that is going to happen! Nothing can stop me from giving thanks to you.

GIVE ME A DRINK

TODAY'S SCRIPTURE

When a Samaritan woman came to draw water, Jesus said to her, "Will you give me a drink?"

JOHN 4:7 (NIV)

This is such an amazing story. Jesus and the disciples were on a journey and in order to reach Galilee, they needed to go through Samaria. Jesus was tired from His journey and the disciples had left to get Him food.

While they were gone, a Samaritan woman came to draw water from the well where Jesus was resting. He said to her, "Give Me a drink," and she replied, "How is it that You, a Jew, asks for a drink from me, a Samaritan woman? For Jews have no dealings with Samaritans" (John 4:7,9).

First, we know that Jesus asked her to bring her husband and she replied that she did not have a husband. So Jesus replied, "For you have had five husbands, and the one whom you now have is not your husband" (John 4:18). The current man was her sixth. Jesus was the seventh and perfect man-encounter that changed her life!

The second point I want to draw out is that Jesus was the one who was thirsty and hungry in this story. He had sent the disciples to get food and He asked the woman for a drink, and yet the only person that got a drink was not Jesus, but the Samaritan woman.

In the meantime, the disciples came back with food encouraging Him to eat. Jesus still had not eaten or had a drink, and yet He turned to the disciples and said to them, "I have food to eat of which you do not know" (John 4:32).

Some people are concerned about taking from Jesus, thinking that He only has so much anointing to share and that it needs to be managed and given out thoughtfully. I have had many people come and ask me to pray for their friend saying, "They need it more than me." I always reply, "Jesus has enough for all!"

Today I want to propose a slightly different approach to how this story ends. I would like to suggest that when we take from Jesus, He actually gets fed too. The more we take from Him, the more He is delighted and the more He gets fed as well!

PERSONAL APPLICATION

1. What can I do to better position myself to see Jesus get fed?

2. Do I act like there is only so much of Jesus' anointing to go around?

3. What can it practically look like this week for me to receive from Jesus?

PRAY THIS TODAY

Jesus, thank you that you delight when I take a drink from you. I pray that you would help me learn to drink from you so that I would be refreshed and stay refreshed. Thank you that there is always enough for everyone and that I don't have to lose out if I share my portion with someone else. Thank you that you are not the God of just enough, you are the God of abundance, the God of more than enough. You are the one that gets fed when I take from you. I am a vessel for your river of life to flow through.

STAYING HUNGRY

TODAY'S SCRIPTURE

Concluding that God was able to raise him up, even from the dead.

HEBREWS 11:19

Hunger and thanksgiving are two sides of the same coin. Staying hungry is an essential part of the journey of staying full of God and flowing in the abundance of Heaven.

One of my favorite Old Testament stories is the story of Abraham and Isaac, first because we see Jesus foreshadowed in the person of Isaac, and second because Abraham was a man that never settled in a place of thanksgiving alone. Abraham was always pushing forward into everything God had for him, even when it was out of his comfort zone.

If we settle in a place of thanksgiving only, as important as thanksgiving is, we will eventually end up leveling out at a place of complacency. And if we only have hunger without thanksgiving, we will be led to frustration, which will lead to desperation, which will lead to unbelief, and eventually unfruitfulness.

Yet hunger and thankfulness together is a dynamic combination. Abraham was not known to have ever settled in one place. He kept pressing forward, past familiarity into what he did not know or understand. We all know the story of God asking Abraham to sacrifice Isaac, and how the angel of the Lord stopped him at the last second. Abraham did not know the end of the story, but he obeyed anyways.

According to Hebrews 11:19, Abraham concluded that even if he sacrificed his son, God would raise him from the dead. Think about this: no one had ever been raised from the dead. It had never been seen. Abraham was surely a man that was thankful, but he was also hungry and had faith for the things he had not yet seen.

PERSONAL APPLICATION

1. Are there areas in my life in which I am thankful for what I've seen, but lost hunger for what I have not yet seen?

2. What areas of impossibility can I intentionally position myself to go after to keep the unfamiliar in front of me?

3. Study the life of Isaac and see how many similarities you can discover between Jesus and Isaac.

4. Take time to dream about breakthroughs that you may never have even thought about.

PRAY THIS TODAY

Father, I thank you that you are the God of breakthrough. I thank you that impossibilities are positioned in front of me so that I can see them bow to the name of Jesus. Help me to never settle for the familiar breakthroughs in life, but to cultivate a pioneering heart that will be stirred to go after the unfamiliar that I have not yet seen.

A NOURISHED SOUL

TODAY'S SCRIPTURE

Then He appointed twelve, that they might be with Him and that He might send them out to preach.

MARK 3:14

George Muller was an incredible missionary that lived in the 1800's. He is well known for his amazing faith in God and feeding over ten thousand orphans. There were times when he had hundreds of orphans to feed, but no food, and yet, he never made a request for financial support. He would prepare the table and have the children sit down to eat in faith. Time and again, just as they were sitting down to the table, there would be a knock at the door, and an unsolicited dinner would be delivered with enough food to feed all the children.

While reading an article on George Muller,[4] there was something in particular that really shook me. He stated, "I

---

[4] "Soul Nourishment First - Pursuing Life Ministries." 2005. 18 Jul. 2016

never study the Word of God to get a message, I study the Word of God to nourish my soul. It's from a nourished soul that I get to feed my people."

While traveling, I meet many people who say to me, "I don't get fed at my church, what am I supposed to do?" My answer to them is always the same. I say, "It's a shepherd's job to lead the sheep, not feed the sheep. Learn to feed yourself."

It's not that we shouldn't get fed at church on Sunday, but many believers only feed themselves once per week. If I fed my physical body the way many believers feed their spirits, I would die of starvation.

In Mark 3:14, we see that Jesus called the disciples first to be with Him, and then to go heal the sick. Notice that the first priority was to be with Him. It was from that place He sent them to heal the sick. Sometimes we get so busy doing things for Him that we forget the core of the Gospel, which is to first be with Him. Most of us have been taught that the priority of the Gospel is to give Him away, but I would like to propose that the first priority of the Gospel is to learn to feed yourself from Him.

I am on over 100 flights a year, but no matter where I am or what airline I fly, there is one thing that is common on every flight. Prior to takeoff, they announce the emergency procedures and say something like, "In the event of an emergency, an oxygen mask will appear in front of you. If you are travelling with a child, put on your own mask first before assisting the child."

While this may seem selfish at first, I propose that this is anything but selfish. If we attend to others before ourselves we could die in the process, and once we are dead we aren't of any good to anyone.

Learn to feed yourself everyday. Not just on Sundays, but feast every day. One way to do this is to listen to nourishing podcasts. You know why it called a "PODcast"? Because it is full of seeds. Another obvious way to feed yourself is to feast on Scripture. George Muller was known for his love of the Word of God and his priority was always to nourish his inner man. There is no way he could have had faith to continually believe that the orphans under his care would be provided for unless he had stayed connected to God through feeding himself.

PERSONAL APPLICATION

1. How can I make time to feed myself?

2. What are some practical steps I can take to better care for the nourishment of my soul?

3. What are some podcasts, books, or other resources that would be nourishing?

4. What can I do to remind myself to be with God and be in the Word on a daily basis?

> **PRAY THIS TODAY**
>
> Father, thank you that I can have a friendship with you. Thank you that I am your friend and that I don't have to work for love. Thank you that I am loved and can't be loved any more than I already am. I pray that you will show me how to feed and nourish my spirit as my first priority. I declare that I am open to the Spirit of God and that I am your friend.

YOU WERE FIRST LOVED

TODAY'S SCRIPTURE

Now there was leaning on Jesus' bosom one of His disciples, whom Jesus loved.

JOHN 13:23

This passage makes me laugh. Who was it that was leaning on the breast of Jesus? It was John. In what book is this passage found? In John. Who wrote the book of John? John wrote it.

So here we have John writing about himself. We can only wonder if the other disciples perhaps thought that Jesus loved John more than them. We know this was not the situation, but I would like to propose that John had a revelation that he was loved, which gave him a sense of security.

This verse is taken from the passage during the Last Supper. The disciples were all present in the Upper Room. Peter turned to John and motioned for him to ask Jesus who will betray Him. And John asked. I always wondered why Peter did not ask Jesus himself. Maybe it was because he could not get near Jesus because of where John was sitting. But perhaps it is because Jesus entrusts secrets to those that are close to His heart.

That night all the disciples left Jesus. The only one that came back to minister to Jesus in His time of need at the foot of the cross was John. I would like to propose that because John focused on how much he was loved, John was the only one able to step out of condemnation from his failure and return to minister to Jesus at His time of need.

Many times we do things for love because we don't know how much we are already loved. We can't be loved anymore than we already are!

Even in our darkest place, He still loves us. In 1 John 4:10 it says, "In this is love, not that we loved God, but that He loved us."

Let your foundation rest in how much you are extravagantly loved. Let your love for Him be an overflow of His love for you. In 1 John 4:19 it says, "We love Him because He first loved us." Stop performing for His love and acceptance and place your attention on just how much you are perfectly loved and already accepted by an incredible Daddy!

PERSONAL APPLICATION

1. On a scale of 1 to 10, 10 being the most, how loved do I feel by God?

2. If Jesus had dinner with me today, would I feel comfortable leaning on His chest?

3. Take a moment right now to ask Jesus to show you how much He loves you and then listen as He tells you how much you are loved.

PRAY THIS TODAY

Father, I thank you that you are an incredible extravagant loving Daddy. I thank you that you have loved me and dreamed about me thousands of years before I was even born. I thank you that you love me with a perfect love, and that even in my bad days you still love me and pursue me. Let me have a greater encounter of your love and kindness and help my foundation to be solid in how much I am loved and already accepted. Help me to love you in return as I receive your love. Thanks Jesus!

GLORIFY HIM AS GOD

TODAY'S SCRIPTURE

Because, although they knew God, they did not glorify Him as God.

ROMANS 1:21

The book of Romans is a book that is full of the power and grace of God. Romans 1:21 sounds negative, but if we look at the opposite of what it's saying, we will find gold. What does the word "glorify" in this verse actually mean? In the Bible, the words glorify, magnify, and thanking God can actually be interchangeable.[8] They mean the same thing.

When we take our eyes off our current situation and look to the Lord with praise and thanksgiving, we glorify and magnify God. We become more aware of who He is in our consciousness. We actually magnify or "make Him bigger" in our consciousness than the issue we are facing.

---

[8] "Strong's Greek: 1392. δοξάζω (doxazó) -- to render or esteem glorious ..." 2013. 18 Jul. 2016

David the Psalmist says in Psalm 34, "Oh magnify the Lord with me and let us exalt His name together." We can't make Him bigger than He already is, but we can certainly change our perspective of how big He actually is. When we magnify the Lord, the issues in our lives are put into their rightful place beneath God. God is larger than any mountain I have yet discovered.

If you are facing what may seem like a mountain of sickness, begin to glorify, magnify, and thank God as your Healer. If you are facing what seems like a mountain of financial issues and lack, then begin to glorify, magnify, and thank God as your Provider. If you are facing the pain of loved ones who are not walking with God, then begin to glorify, magnify, and thank God as the Restorer and Savior. What seems like a mountain of sickness, financial issues, or loss will begin to morph into a small hill when you glorify, magnify, and thank God focusing on His immensity.

When you give your attention to Him as the answer, fear of lack and loss will begin to dissolve. Strength, wisdom, and the grace of God will begin to supernaturally overcome every obstacle you encounter.

There have been many situations in my life when I have been overwhelmed by the circumstances I faced. It has always been a strong reminder that I have taken my eyes off the answer, making the problem larger than the answer, Jesus! When I shift my attention back to glorifying, magnifying, and thanking God for what He has done and is doing, my heart and mind can realign to how big my God is and how small the issue at hand really is.

PERSONAL APPLICATION

1. What challenges in my life have I glorified instead of glorifying God?

2. What are two practical ways that I can remove my "magnifying glass" from the issue and place it on the answer?

OVERFLOW

3. Is there someone who can keep me accountable to magnifying God instead of the obstacles I encounter? Have a conversation with that person soon about this and come up with a plan of action to keep each other accountable.

PRAY THIS TODAY

Father, thank you that you are the answer to every situation. Thank you that nothing is too difficult for you. There is no situation that you are not bigger than. You are the God of more than enough. You created the universe with your words. Nothing takes you by surprise. You are trustworthy, and right now I choose to put my attention on you alone.

ROYAL AMBASSADORS FOR CHRIST

TODAY'S SCRIPTURE

Now then, we are ambassadors for Christ.

2 CORINTHIANS 5:20

You have an incredible job in the Kingdom of God. In fact, the job that you have is esteemed, celebrated, and high ranking. You actually have the backing of Heaven behind you, to protect, defend, and help you. Heaven is waiting to act on your behalf, because you are an ambassador for Christ to this world.

According to 2 Corinthians 5:20, we are heavenly delegates or ambassadors who have been sent forth as representatives from Heaven to planet earth.

No one in the Kingdom is unimportant to the plan of God. We actually represent Jesus to the world around us. As ambassadors of Christ, we get to walk in the delegated power and authority of His precious blood. We have access to the resources of Heaven to back us.

We are no longer orphans; we have been adopted into the family of God. God calls us sons and daughters. Just like a son or a daughter can represent their father because they have the same family name and DNA, so we can represent our Father because we are in His family. God doesn't just want to use us like servants. Out of His heart of love He chooses to entrust us with His authority.

Next time you feel unimportant, I want you to stop and take a moment to think about who you really are in Jesus. You are in Him and He is in you. You are a royal ambassador, representing the King of Kings and fully backed by the power and the resources of Heaven.

PERSONAL APPLICATION

1. Do I view myself as an ambassador for Christ?

2. What does a successful ambassador do? In what ways can I model what a successful ambassador would do for Christ?

3. Do I view myself as a son/daughter and a prince/princess of God?

4. Ask Jesus to give you a picture of who you are to Him both as an ambassador and a son/prince/daughter/princess. Draw or paint out what He shows you.

PRAY THIS TODAY

I thank you, Father, that I am no longer an orphan; I am a son/daughter of God. As a son/daughter of God, I am an ambassador of Heaven representing Jesus Christ. Thank you that I have an important job in the Kingdom to be myself and represent you. So I open my heart to you and I remind myself that I am an ambassador of the King Himself. I am royalty. I am a prince/princess of the of King. Thank you that you are in me and I am in you.

YOU ARE NOT A VICTIM

TODAY'S SCRIPTURE

Having disarmed principalities and powers, He made a public spectacle of them, triumphing over them in it.

COLOSSIANS 2:15

We are not victims! We are victors because of the blood of Jesus. If you read the end of the Bible you will see we win. Because of Jesus' death on the cross and His glorious resurrection from the dead, the forces of hell have already been defeated.

We need to understand the truth. The demonic forces of hell have been legally stripped of their authority and are defeated. You are not a weak Christian who is learning to cope with the devil's attacks. You are not a Christian who is trying to survive. You can thrive and destroy the works of the devil! Because of the power of the blood of Jesus, He has already won the victory.

OVERFLOW

In Colossians 2:15 when it declares that Jesus triumphed over evil powers, it is explicitly declaring that Jesus took the enemy apart piece by piece as He thoroughly "disarmed principalities and powers." When Jesus was finished with the demonic forces, they were utterly plundered.

Satan is not a force that we are trying to defeat; He is already defeated. Because we often walk around like victims, not knowing how to effectively use our God-given authority, Satan illegally operates, destroying people and creation.

I have not yet met an issue that is bigger than Jesus. Jesus victoriously plundered the enemy when He rose from the dead. When you take a look in the mirror, learn to see yourself as one who already has the victory. You already have the authority that is necessary to keep the enemy under your feet, right where he belongs. You are not the victim, you are the victor, because of the precious blood of Jesus!

PERSONAL APPLICATION

1. Are there some areas in my life where the enemy has been illegally operating and where I need to exercise my God-given authority as a victor?

2. Is there an area of my life that seems too big for Jesus to handle? If there is, ask God for His perspective on the matter and surrender it to Him.

OVERFLOW

3. What thought patterns, words, and attitudes do I need to change to act like a victor instead of a victim?

PRAY THIS TODAY

Father, I thank you for the precious powerful blood of Jesus. I declare it is by your blood that I am no longer a victim, but the victor. I am the head, I am no longer the tail. I was designed to be victorious and to rule and reign in life. I thank you that the enemy has no authority over my life and I never have to settle for defeat. When I look in the mirror, I see someone who has already won the victory. I already have the necessary authority to keep the enemy under my feet, right where he belongs. Thank you for renewing my thinking and enabling me to be victorious in every situation.

ALIVE TO CHRIST

TODAY'S SCRIPTURE

I have been crucified with Christ; it is no longer I who live, but Christ lives in me.

GALATIANS 2:20

The most common question I get asked is, "Why don't I see miracles happen through me?" I love the power of the cross because Christ did not just die for us, He actually died as us. When we were born again, we were co-crucified with Christ and the "I" in us was crucified with Christ. Our "I" is actually dead, dead, dead, dead.

But the best part is that Christ lives in us! Not only were we co-crucified with Christ, but we were also co-resurrected with Him. The "I" in us died and was co-resurrected as "we": Him in us and us in Him. So to answer the question, "Why don't I see miracles happen through me?" It's because, it's not about the "I" in you, it's about Christ. 100% of Christ in and though 100% of you. We are no longer "I", we became "we" when we were united with Christ.

Many of us wonder why we struggle with a life of bondage and sin after we are born again. The reality of why we struggle isn't that we still have an active sinful nature; it's because we've been taught that we have an active sinful nature and are dying to sin. As long as we believe that we are dying to sin and our sinful nature, instead of realizing that we are dead to it, we will not be alive in Christ. How can we live like Christ, if we believe we are dying daily?

A person who believes they are dying daily will actually sin by faith. Have you ever seen a dead person get out of a coffin and sin? The good news of the Gospel is that we are not only dead to sin, but alive to Christ Jesus.

PERSONAL APPLICATION

1. Is there is an area in my life where I am struggling with sin? What do I believe about that sin?

2. Do I believe it is possible to live the Christian life without walking in my old sin nature?

DECLARE THIS TODAY

I declare that I have been crucified with Christ, my old sinful nature is dead. It is no longer a part of me. I am fully alive in Christ. I have been completely made new. I walk in righteousness and purity because Christ lives in me.

ALLOW ADVERSITY TO FUEL YOUR FIRE

TODAY'S SCRIPTURE

Only do not rebel against the Lord, nor fear the people of the land, for they are our bread; their protection has departed from them and the Lord is with us. Do not fear them.

NUMBERS 14:9

Someone came up to me at a healing conference recently and said, "It must be easy for you to fuel your fire, as you see miracles all the time." I replied, "Absolutely, when I see a miracle, it is like fuel on my fire, but I am also likely to see more people not healed than you too." When someone is healed, it is fuel on my fire, but when someone is not healed, it is also fuel on my fire. Yet when many of us face adversity or defeat, we feel like it's having a bucket of cold water thrown on us.

I love the story of Joshua and Caleb. The Bible tells us that they had a different kind of spirit. The heads of the twelve tribes of the children of Israel plus Joshua were sent to spy out the land in Numbers 13. Eleven came back with a bad report: "The land through which we have gone as spies is a land that devours its inhabitants, and all the people whom we saw in it are men of great stature. There we saw the giants (the descendants of Anak came from the giants)."

Joshua and Caleb came back in Numbers 13:30 with a good report: "Let us go up at once and take possession, for we are well able to overcome it." They go on to say in Numbers 14:9, "Only do not rebel against the Lord, nor fear the people of the land, for they are our bread; their protection has departed from them, and the Lord is with us. Do not fear them."

Joshua and Caleb were referring to the adversities that they were about to encounter and while they did not deny that the adversities existed, they treated them as food. We can either complain about trials and disappointments we face, or we can also be of a different spirit and use them as food to strengthen our faith on this journey.

When we complain, we often end up going around the same mountain again. Friends, enemies and adversities will come. How much stronger would we be if we used our adversities as food to strengthen our faith and walk with God? I want to challenge you to not only allow your breakthroughs, but also your disappointments to fuel your fire so that in whatever circumstance you find yourself, you will always be burning.

PERSONAL APPLICATION

1. What kind of report do I give when I face an obstacle that looks like it could keep me from God's promises being fulfilled in my life?

2. What are a few practical ways that I can turn adversities into food to nourish and strengthen me?

3. How can I change my mindset to be like Caleb and Joshua, who believed the report of the Lord?

DECLARE THIS TODAY

I declare that nothing will stop me from entering into God's promises for my life. Every situation and circumstance that looks like an obstacle, I will overcome! If God says the land is mine, I choose to believe the land is mine. I choose to take every adversity as food to allow it to strengthen my resolve. I will continue to move forward. I will be victorious.

COVERED IN THE BLOOD

TODAY'S SCRIPTURE

Also for Adam and his wife the Lord God made tunics of skin, and clothed them.

GENESIS 3:21

When Adam and Eve sinned they became aware of their nakedness "and they sewed fig leaves together and made themselves coverings" (Genesis 3:7). God came into the garden in the cool of the day looking for Adam and Eve, but they hid themselves from His presence.

When you do a word study on the word "coverings"[5] in Genesis 3:7, you'll find that it means: "a waistcloth or belt." A waistcloth was a partial covering, enough to cover the bare essentials. So Adam and Eve used fig leaves to partially cover themselves. The fig leaf represents our self-righteousness. Adam and Eve, in their sin, attempted to cover themselves

---

[5] "Strong's Hebrew: 2290. חֲגוֹר (chagowr) - apron - Bible Hub." 2013. 18 Jul. 2016

with self-righteousness. Yet, no matter how much self-righteousness we use to cover ourselves, it will never be enough.

Often we attempt to hide from God in our sin, dressed in our self-righteousness, and yet God wants us to come to Him as we are. Adam and Eve came before God in Genesis 3:21 and "He made tunics of skin and clothed them."

The tunic of skin was taken from an animal, which is believed to be that of a lamb.

When the skin was taken off the lamb, there would have been a lot of bloodshed.

God took the skin off the animal and placed it over Adam and Eve. They would have either literally or figuratively been covered in the blood of the lamb.

Friends, let's stop trying to dress ourselves in self-righteousness and recognize that God has a better option. We are fully covered in His righteousness; we are covered in the blood of the Lamb!

God is not impressed with our attempts at self-righteousness or our attempts to cover our sin. It can't be done. Let's stop performing and recognize that it's only by His righteousness that we are covered in the precious blood of Jesus and can stand blameless and spotless before Him.

When Jesus cursed the fig tree in Mark 11:14, I wonder if He was cursing self-righteousness. When we surrender to God, we get covered in His righteousness, which is a far better option than being dressed in fig leaves.

PERSONAL APPLICATION

1. Do I dress myself in self-righteousness or allow myself to be covered by Jesus' righteousness? How can I stop dressing myself in self-righteousness and simply accept the righteousness of Jesus?

2. Do I sometimes hide from God because of shame? What can I do if this happens again?

3. Find a song that speaks about the blood of Jesus and as you listen to it, meditate on and thank Jesus for everything that His blood purchased for you on the cross.

DECLARE THIS TODAY

I am the righteousness of God in Christ Jesus. My sins have been covered by the blood. Jesus became sin for me so that I could become the righteousness of Christ. I am pure and spotless before God.

YOU ARE A NEW CREATION

TODAY'S SCRIPTURE

Therefore, if anyone is in Christ, he is a new creation; old things have passed away; behold, all things have become new.

2 CORINTHIANS 5:17

When we become Christians we become a brand new creation in Christ. The old things in our lives are gone, and everything is new. A brand new creation is not a fixed up old creation.

    I heard an analogy that coming to Christ is like coming before Him on a broken bike. The tires are flat, the spokes are bent, the seat is twisted, and the paint is falling off and Jesus pumps up the tires, fixes the spokes, straightens the seat, and gives us a new coat of paint. However, if we think about our lives like that, we wouldn't be a brand new creation; we would be a fixed up old creation.

According to Scripture, we are a brand new creation. "Old things have passed away; behold, all things have become new" (2 Corinthians 5:17). I would like to propose in this analogy that we come to Christ dressed in figs leaves on a broken bike and we leave wearing pure white linen clothes in a F1 McLaren sports car.

Why is this so important to understand? Because our past does not define us! Our past does not define our future. Christ is the one that commands our destiny. Many of us live in the past, dwelling on things for which have already been forgiven. We hold on to guilt and shame and spend so much time looking into the past to figure out what is wrong with us today. I am here to say there is nothing wrong with us, but there could be something wrong with how we think. We are an entirely brand new creation that still needs a transformation of the mind.

Our "old man" or sinful nature has passed away. I would like to propose that many people who spend too much time looking into their past, are actually examining the old man, who has already been co-crucified. Our sinful nature is dead. When there are things in the past that need to be dealt with, never go there without Jesus, your attorney, present.

Once we get a clear revelation of who we are in Christ and that He commands our future and destiny, we will begin to live victoriously and be able to let go of past regrets, shame, and guilt. Only then can we begin to walk into the abundant life of which Jesus spoke.

PERSONAL APPLICATION

1. Do I see myself dressed in white linen (pure and spotless) and driving a fancy sports car or do I see myself dressed in fig leaves (tainted and shabby) and riding a fixed up bicycle?

2. Are there areas from my past life that I have allowed to define me? How does Jesus see those areas of my life?

3. How can I transform my mind to believe who I am in Christ?

DECLARE THIS TODAY

Father, thank you that I am who you say I am. I thank you that I am not defined by my past; I am defined and commanded into my destiny by You! Thank you that at the cross you took my shame, guilt, and condemnation, so that I can walk in an overflowing abundant life. Jesus, I choose to align myself to your Word, not my past. I ask for a greater revelation of the truth of who I am in you and who you are in me! Thank you that I am a brand new creation.

FIND YOUR CONTENTMENT IN CHRIST

TODAY'S SCRIPTURE

Not that I speak in regard to need, for I have learned in whatever state I am, to be content.

PHILIPPIANS 4:11

I have met many Christians that, frankly, are not living the abundant life of Jesus. We all want breakthrough in our lives, whether it's in health, finances, relationships, or another area. I am the first to acknowledge that I want to see increased breakthrough in many areas of my life.

However, if we are only content once we actually receive our breakthrough, we will end up living miserable and unhappy lives until we receive it. I love to see people believe for and then receive incredible breakthroughs in every area of life, yet we need to be careful that our contentment is not contingent on our breakthrough.

The apostle Paul said, "I have learned in whatever state I

am, to be content" (Philippians 4:11). This is a man that had incredible ups and downs in his life. He saw the blessing and breakthroughs of God, but was also beaten, shipwrecked, and thrown in prison, yet he was content.

If you need to see breakthrough before you live in contentment, it will drain you of abundant life. You will find yourself always looking for peace and joy in the future, instead of finding it in today in your present circumstance.

In the midst of your current circumstance Jesus is with you. In the ups and the downs, He is right there next to you. Learn to discover the joy of finding Him in your situation. In the down times, look for something for which you can be thankful. You can also thank God for the breakthrough that is coming and engage your faith. Since God lives outside of time, what would it look like to give thanks for your breakthroughs believing they have already happened?

I encourage you to live in contentment because you have Jesus!

PERSONAL APPLICATION

1. What breakthroughs am I believing for in my life?

2. Am I waiting to be content and happy until after my breakthrough comes?

3. List three ways you can find contentment while waiting for breakthrough.

4. Take a moment to thank God for your breakthrough that is coming.

PRAY THIS TODAY

Jesus, thank you that you are the source of my joy and happiness. I choose to be content while waiting for more breakthrough in my life. I no longer want my emotions tossed to and fro depending on my circumstances. Thank you that you are always good and that I can find you in the midst of every situation.

KEEP YOUR ATTENTION ON JESUS

TODAY'S SCRIPTURE

Looking unto Jesus, the author and finisher of our faith.
HEBREWS 12:2

In over 16 years in ministry, I have had some real ups and downs. For a large part of my earlier public ministry, it was a battle to even keep myself encouraged and I often found myself in a state of depression. I use to get introspective thinking there must be something incredibly wrong with me.

I finally discovered one of the greatest keys to living encouraged and staying in the overflow of Heaven. I discovered that I can remain encouraged every day if I simply put my attention and affection on this one thing: keeping my focus on what God has done and is doing.

I can't afford to put my attention on the things that have not happened. When I am feeling down, I can now quickly recognize it's because I have taken my attention off the good reports and shifted it to the things that have not yet happened.

When we put our attention on negative reports, we begin to exalt the negative report or problem. And when we exalt the problem, we create the problem in our minds to be larger than the answer.

I have learned that I need to be more answer-focused. The more I focus on the answer, the less impressive the darkness becomes. At the end of the day, darkness is not the problem. Darkness is purely the absence of light. So if I can keep answer-focused I will find myself, by default, living in the light. The light alone dispels darkness!

Always look for something to celebrate. I know, for myself, there are so many areas in which I still need breakthrough, and yet I'm learning to keep my attention on what has happened and what is happening, to keep me encouraged.

Stop exalting the darkness and the problems and start to exalt and magnify the answer. I have yet to find a problem that is larger than the ultimate answer: JESUS!

PERSONAL APPLICATION

1. Do I tend to be more discouraged or encouraged on a day-to-day basis?

2. What have I been focusing on lately?

3. Have I been dwelling on anything negative recently? If so, what is God's truth about the situation?

4. What can I do to remind myself to keep my eyes on the answer daily?

5. List five good things that are happening in your life right now and choose to give thanks for them every day this week.

PRAY THIS TODAY

Father, thank you that good things are happening in my life right now. Help me to learn to celebrate and give thanks daily for what you are doing in my life. I declare that you are the answer to every situation I face, no matter how big or small. I choose to trust you and to keep my eyes focused on Jesus.

TIME FOR AN OIL CHANGE?

TODAY'S SCRIPTURE

And the foolish said to the wise, "Give us some of your oil, for our lamps are going out."

MATTHEW 25:8

My car requires an oil change every 7,000 miles. While my car was getting serviced one day, I sensed the Lord say that my life is similar to my car. If I don't get my car serviced, the oil will become sludgy and dirty and my car won't run at its maximum efficiency and will eventually create long-term damage. He went on to say that it is the same in our lives. We need to keep our oil fresh and topped up.

Yet many of us go for excessively long periods without ever having the oil of our lives changed or checked. We end up becoming sludgy and slow and the flame begins to burn dimly. We often end up going from one touch of God until we are burned out, then desperately look for the next. Wouldn't it be amazing if we did not have to go from one touch of the

Holy Spirit to the next, but we actually got to operate in the fullness of the Holy Spirit at all times?

We have a choice to either be one of the wise or one of the foolish virgins. In the story of Matthew 25, the foolish virgins took their lamps, but no oil with them. The wise virgins, on the other hand, took oil and their lamps.

Matthew 25:5-9 tells us, "But while the bridegroom was delayed, they all slumbered and slept. And at midnight a cry was heard: 'Behold the bridegroom is coming; go out to meet him!' Then all those virgins arose and trimmed their lamps. And the foolish said to the wise, 'Give us some of your oil, for our lamps are going out.' But the wise answered, saying, 'No, lest there should not be enough for us and you; but go rather to those who sell, and buy for yourselves.'"

While I love coming into the momentum that someone else has created, it's important that we don't always run on other people's oil. We should learn to carry enough of our own oil to bring us through the longest and darkest nights. I don't want to go from touch to touch of the Holy Spirit; I want to operate in the fullness of the Spirit by carrying plenty of oil to burn bright.

If you feel slow, sludgy, or that your flame is dimly burning, the best thing that you can do is have an oil change. Get rid of the dirty oil, and be topped up with fresh clean oil. I would like to propose the best thing you can do is to have the sump plug removed so your oil never has a chance to get sludgy and dirty. Instead it will always be flowing, leaking out over everything in which you come into contact.

TIME FOR AN OIL CHANGE?

PERSONAL APPLICATION

1. Do I need an oil change or top up?

2. When I am feeling dry or empty, what do I do to get refilled with the Holy Spirit's oil?

3. How can I keep the oil of the Holy Spirit continually flowing in my life so I can operate in His fullness?

OVERFLOW

> **PRAY THIS TODAY**
>
> Father, I thank you that you never want me to run out of oil. You desire that I always have fresh oil with oil to spare. I pray that you will give me insight into how I can walk in the fullness of the Spirit, so that my oil will never get sludgy or dirty. I want my flame to burn brighter and brighter, never burning out.

WANT TO BE LIKE A GIANT?

TODAY'S SCRIPTURE

As newborn babes, desire the pure milk of the word, that you may grow thereby.

1 PETER 2:2

I meet many believers that want to do extraordinary things for God and feel they are called to be giants in the Kingdom of God. I want us to ponder two things today. The first is that becoming a giant is a process. I have yet to see a baby born as a giant, although I have seen a baby born knowing their destiny is to grow into a giant. Learn to enjoy the process of growing, because growing is a process.

The second and main point I want to focus on is that if you want to become a giant, you must eat like a giant. Giants don't become giants by eating small portions. Giants become giants because they know how to feed themselves. They eat, eat, and eat. I'm not talking about eating in the physical, but about feasting on the Word of God and what God is doing and has done.

This is hardly a revelation, but in the natural when you eat, you get full. That is not how it works in the Kingdom though. In the Kingdom, the more you eat the hungrier you become. The more I see the Kingdom, the more I want the Kingdom, and the hungrier I get. The hungrier I get, the more I must eat, and the more I eat, the more I grow.

This is the incredible journey of becoming a giant. So how do you keep growing? Eat a lot and place yourself in a position of praying for impossibilities. Knowing that as believers, we each have the answer for these impossibilities inside of us, we need to learn to live out of that abundance. In doing so, we will end up growing by what we learn, both when things go right and when things go wrong.

Whether you see breakthrough or not, take the opportunity to feed yourself from the lesson and grow. Don't beat yourself up for what went wrong, but feed and grow. I've never seen someone grow physically overnight or grow by simply eating one meal. It is from a constant supply of feeding on the Word, feeding from your experiences, taking risks, and learning that growth is a process.

We can stay full of God, by eating and learning that growth is a process, both in the agony of defeat and the delight of breakthrough.

PERSONAL APPLICATION

1. Do I eat by placing myself in front of impossible situations and taking risk?

2. Am I embracing the process of becoming a spiritual giant or am I impatient?

3. Who do I consider a giant and what does becoming a spiritual giant look like to me?

4. What do I need to feed myself on in order to grow?

> **PRAY THIS TODAY**
>
> Father, I pray that you would increase my desire to feast on you and your Word. I want to make you the priority in my life and not just "eat" whenever I have time. It's my desire to grow and mature in you and I know the only way to do that is to nourish my spirit. I want to feast on You!

SEEKING THE KINGDOM

by *MARY WEBB*
Intern to Chris Gore 2016

TODAY'S SCRIPTURE

But seek first the Kingdom of God and His righteousness, and all these things shall be added to you.

MATTHEW 6:33

One evening, after a long day of air travel, I finally arrived at my hotel room. I fell into bed exhausted and quickly fell asleep. I awoke the next morning and began to pray for my church back home, remembering it was the time they would be gathering for a weekly prayer meeting. I had been praying a short while when my phone rang. It was a number I did not recognize. When I answered, the gentleman on the other end said to me, "Ma'am, this is security at the airport and I believe I may have something that belongs to you. I have a laptop computer and the bag has your name and number on it."

I quickly turned on the light in the room and walked over to where I had placed my bags the evening before. Sure enough, my computer bag was missing! The gentleman on the phone went on to say that at about 6:00am he saw the bag sitting in a chair unattended. He observed the bag for awhile and it appeared not to belong to anyone around. This is when he read the claim tag and gave me a call. Stunned, I thanked him and told him I would be in to claim it ASAP.

I began to process the fact that I had left the airport at about 11:00pm the night before. The computer bag had been sitting in the chair for about seven hours before the security guard found it untouched and unharmed. As I stood in the hotel room that morning, I sensed the Lord say that as we focus on His Kingdom, He is taking care of our needs (even ones we don't know about), and will work everything out for our good.

In Scripture, we find that Jesus perfectly exemplifies seeking the Kingdom first. In John 5:19, Jesus says, "Most assuredly, I say to you, the Son can do nothing of Himself, but what He sees the Father do; for whatever He does, the Son also does in a like manner." In Jeremiah 29:13 we are given the beautiful promise, "you will seek Me and find Me, when you search for Me with all your heart." As we are seeking the Kingdom we will find it.

God knows our every need and His resources are unlimited. Our job is to seek first the Kingdom.

PERSONAL APPLICATION

1. What does "seek first the Kingdom" look like in my daily life? Am I intentionally taking time each day to pursue relationship with my heavenly Father?

2. In what ways could I structure my life to prioritize seeking the Kingdom of God before all else?

3. What stories do I have of God supernaturally taking care of my needs supernaturally?

> **PRAY THIS TODAY**
>
> Father, you have purposed and fashioned me to seek your Kingdom first. I dedicate my mind, body, and spirit to seek your face. I trust in your promise that where I seek you with my whole heart I will find you. I thank you that you know my every need, and I declare that you are good. Thank you so much for all the times you have taken care of my needs supernaturally. Place within me today a supernatural tenacity and faith to stay fixed on your Kingdom. I align my thoughts to Heaven's agenda and delight in knowing you have promised you will work everything for good in my life.

A THANKFUL HEART

by *MARY WEBB*
Intern to Chris Gore 2016

TODAY'S SCRIPTURE

In everything give thanks; for this is the will of God in Christ Jesus for you.

1 THESSALONIANS 5:18

Have you ever noticed that it's almost impossible to be thankful and depressed at the same time? Thanksgiving gives us a higher perspective and fosters an atmosphere of expectation in our hearts. Scripture tells us that we, "Enter into His gates with thanksgiving, and into His courts with praise" (Psalm 100:4). What a powerful promise this is. Do you realize that as you begin to celebrate the goodness of God and to thank Him for all He has done and is doing that you are actually entering into a higher realm? Giving thanks to God and celebrating the people around us positively changes the atmosphere.

When we begin to celebrate the goodness of God and His faithfulness in our lives it creates an atmosphere of

OVERFLOW

expectation and faith. In Scripture, we see Jesus giving thanks for the five loaves of bread and two fish just before they are multiplied. "Taking the five loaves and the two fish and looking up to heaven, he gave thanks and broke the loaves" (Matthew 14:19 NIV). In His looking up to Heaven we see Him turning His thoughts not to what He was holding in His hands at that present moment, but to His heavenly Father. As we turn our eyes to our Father and give thanks for what we have, we will often see it multiplied.

We never want to do something out of a formula, in other words, doing something because we think it will cause something else to happen. That is called manipulation. However, there are foundational principles in the Bible that are meant to instruct us in the way we should live. One principle we see Jesus consistently demonstrating is a lifestyle of thankfulness. Thankfulness and the Kingdom are inseparable.

We are exhorted in 1 Thessalonians 5:18 to give thanks in everything. Have you ever wondered how it is possible to be thankful in challenging situations? We only need to look to Jesus for a demonstration of this. Before Jesus went to the cross He gave thanks. Imagine that. Scripture tells us that He endured the cross for the "joy set that was before Him" (Hebrews 12:2). We find Jesus demonstrating an eternal mindset. His thanks was not based on His present circumstances. His thanks was based on what was coming as a result of the cross, and this gave Him joy. His focus in that moment was not on the pain of the cross; it was on the joy that was set before Him!

We get to partake of this joy as well because we have been made heirs of the Kingdom with Jesus (Romans 8:17). We can look at trials with a new perspective if we can embrace thankfulness. As we begin to give God thanks and recognize all He has done and is doing in our lives, it actually positions us for breakthrough.

PERSONAL APPLICATION

1. What are some ways I can intentionally practice thankfulness in my life daily?

2. Am I keeping a thankful perspective like Jesus in all situations and circumstances?

OVERFLOW

3. How can I communicate to the people around me my thankfulness for them?

PRAY THIS TODAY

Father, I thank you for your son, Jesus Christ, and I thank you that through Him I now have an eternal perspective through which to view all areas of my life. Today I choose to be thankful in all things. Open my eyes to a heavenly perspective of all that I have been given. I choose to turn my eyes to you, knowing that you are always good. Cultivate within me a thankful heart that is quick to recognize blessing. Father, let me be one who takes an atmosphere of thankfulness everywhere I go, and let that atmosphere be contagious to the ones around me.

OVERFLOWING WITH JESUS

by *CLEMENT SIM*
Intern to Chris Gore 2016

TODAY'S SCRIPTURE

The thief does not come except to steal, and to kill, and to destroy. I have come that they may have life, and that they may have it more abundantly.

JOHN 10:10

Have you ever poured a glass of water for a guest or been served a glass of water in a restaurant? Did you realize that the glass is never completely full as there is alway space for it to be filled up more? A glass is never completely full until it is overflowing with water. When it is overflowing, there is no more space to be filled and the glass is completely full. When you touch the glass, your hand will be wet because of the overflow of water. It is the same in the Kingdom. We are never completely full until we are overflowing with God so that anyone who encounters us encounters the overflow of God. You are overflowing because you have the fullness of God in you. When anyone touches you, they encounter the overflow of God!

OVERFLOW

Since becoming a believer, I have heard many preachers quote John 10:10. However, many have used this verse to illustrate the devil's mode of operation in our lives, "to kill, steal and destroy" us. Sound familiar? One day, when I came to this verse in my Bible, God said, "Clement, stop reading the verse in parts. The Bible is to reveal the heart of our Savior, never the heart of the devil." Something stirred in my spirit to continue reading the rest of the verse about Jesus giving life.

The Holy Spirit began to highlight two words, which led me to study them deeper. The Greek word for "life" (zōē)[6] means: "the state of one who is possessed of vitality, absolute fulness of life". It is the divine life of God, uniquely possessed by God, or absolute fullness of life. The Greek word for "abundantly" (perissos)[7] means: "over and above, excessive, more than is necessary."

Jesus does not want us to simply know our access to His divine life, He wants us to know the overflow. In this sense, we are not just a carrier of God's presence, but a carrier of the overflow of His divine life.

Interestingly, John 7:38 talks about a river of living water that flows from every believer. A river is a natural phenomenon as the water always flows. Living in the overflow of Jesus' abundant life is not passive; it is like a river that never stops flowing. This is a picture of naturally overflowing with the divine life. Our job is simply to connect with Jesus.

---

[6] "Zoe - New Testament Greek Lexicon - New American Standard." 2009. 18 Jul. 2016

[7] "Perissos - New Testament Greek Lexicon - New American Standard." 2009. 18 Jul. 2016

Remember the day you received Jesus into your life as your Lord and Savior? At that very moment, Jesus, the source of the divine life, took residence in you and you began to overflow with divine life. Whether or not you can feel or sense it, that river of overflowing life is always within you. The last time I checked the Bible, Lazarus was raised from the dead when Jesus walked in, overflowing with His life. How much more can we release Jesus' life in every situation and environment when we recognize the river that is flowing from within us?

PERSONAL APPLICATION

1. Am I like the overflowing glass that has no more space to be filled? Why?

2. Have I been reading the Bible to understand the heart of my Savior?

3. How can I remind myself that I am a river that never stops flowing with life?

4. Into what situations can I release Jesus' overflowing divine life?

PRAY THIS TODAY

Father, I thank you that you sent Jesus to give us divine life that is overflowing. Thank you for making me a river that overflows with your life that can change every dead situation or environment. I want to recognize the river of life that is within me, not based on how I feel but based on your truth and the cross. Today, I will be an encounter of life for someone else's life or situation. I never stop flowing and I am never dry.

LIVING IN THE FULLNESS OF HEAVEN

by *CLEMENT SIM*
Intern to Chris Gore 2016

TODAY'S SCRIPTURE

Now when He was asked by the Pharisees when the kingdom of God would come, He answered them and said, "The kingdom of God does not come with observation; nor will they say, 'See here!' or 'See there!' For indeed, the kingdom of God is within you."

LUKE 17:20-21

Growing up, I was a curious boy, always wanting to find things out for myself instead of hearing about them from others. There is nothing quite like a first-hand experience to learn things. For example, I had been told several times not to touch a hot iron. One day, I decided to touch it anyway and I learned the hard way. Another incident was when I learned that metal conducts electricity. You might be able to guess what I did. I put a metal object into the wall socket and literally got the shock of my life.

OVERFLOW

We cannot deny the existence of something just because we cannot see it with our physical eyes. Both heat and electricity are things I couldn't see. Even though I couldn't see them, they still existed. Jesus said that the Kingdom of God is within us through the Holy Spirit. I personally have not seen the Holy Spirit with my physical eyes, but that does not mean He does not live in me. Romans 14:17 says, "The kingdom of God is not eating or drinking, but righteousness and peace and joy in the Holy Spirit." We do not have a limited portion of the Spirit; we have Him without measure.

When I first heard the gospel, my main impression was that Jesus came to give us a ticket to Heaven. It was like Jesus was handing out tickets to those who would respond and people would line up to get ahold of this unique opportunity. Funny as it may seem, that was the picture that ran through my mind. Now having a deeper understanding of the Gospel, I realize that Jesus did not just come to give us a ticket to Heaven. He went through everything, from the cross to His resurrection, so that He can put Heaven within us. Now that's a whole different game plan! We are not waiting to use our ticket to enter Heaven; we already have Heaven inside of us.

Now, back to my childhood experience. We cannot see the heating rod in an iron, but it is within the iron for a purpose. Its job is to heat the iron and so it can function the way it was designed. Similarly, the Kingdom of God is within us for a purpose. It was God's idea and design to have the fullness of Heaven dwell in us through the Holy Spirit. Now, we can be empowered and function beyond our own limitations.

Just like a wall socket, we cannot see the current, but the power is still inside. It only needs the right connection to tap into its power. Similarly, the Kingdom of God is power flowing within us. When we know that the connection to the power is Jesus, it will flow through us and transform everything we touch.

We are to live by faith, not by sight. The Kingdom is already within us, even when we can't see it. Our role is not to get more of Heaven into us; Jesus already did that. We already received the fullness when we said "Yes" to Jesus. I would like to propose that our job is to always stay connected to the source: Jesus. When we release Heaven, we replace joy for mourning, health for sickness, and abundance for lack. We can release the atmosphere of Heaven on earth because the Kingdom of God fully dwells in us.

PERSONAL APPLICATION

1. What are some areas in life that I need to start recognizing by faith and not by sight?

2. What is the purpose for the Kingdom to be within me?

3. How can I tap into and release the power of God's Kingdom daily?

4. What aspect of the Kingdom does God want me to release today?

PRAY THIS TODAY

Father, I thank you that you sent Jesus to give us the Kingdom. I am not waiting to get into Heaven; I already have Heaven inside me. I am a child of God that lives by faith on what the Word of God says and not by what I can see. Because the Kingdom of God is within me, I attract angelic activities, signs, and wonders on a daily basis. No matter where I go, people can encounter the atmosphere of Heaven because of me.

THINK YOURSELF HAPPY

TODAY'S SCRIPTURE

I think myself happy, King Agrippa, because today I shall answer for myself before you concerning all the things of which I am accused by the Jews.

ACTS 26:2

In a day when there is so much turbulence going on around us through wars, the economy, politics, sickness, and what appears to be chaos in general, we need to make sure that we don't allow external circumstances to determine our inner joy. If we are only going to be joyful when all is well in the world, we will be likely to lead a pretty miserable life.

Paul was facing a stressful situation when he was on trial and yet in his address to King Agrippa, which became known as Paul's longest, He begins by saying, "I think myself happy, King Agrippa." How often do we, as believers, become victims of our circumstances? Sure, we will walk in joy in seasons, but how often do we let the circumstances surrounding our lives and the world determine our joy? What would it look like we we discovered that joy is simply an inside job? What would it look like if, regardless of the chaos around us, we refused to let it alter our joy barometer? Regardless of the season we are in, whether or not there is chaos in the world or we are facing tough personal circumstances, joy is just a mindset-change away.

In my journey into joy, I was complaining one day to one of my seniors leaders about my personal circumstances. I told him I didn't feel like I had a life at the moment. With a loving fatherly rebuke, I was reminded that the situation I was presently in was my life. He went on to say that if I was going to wait until my circumstances changed, life would pass me by and I would be miserable, spinning, with no feeling of control. That was a lesson I had already learned, but I found myself going around that mountain once again, having become the victim of my circumstances. It was a refreshing wake-up call. Despite my circumstances I need to make the most of my life within my current circumstances because joy is an inside job.

PERSONAL APPLICATION

1. What circumstances have I become a victim to that have caused me to lose my inner joy?

2. What mindsets can I change, despite the circumstances not changing?

3. What places in my life have I lost thankfulness?

OVERFLOW

4. How can I recalibrate my life to a place of inner joy?

> **PRAY THIS TODAY**
>
> Father, thank you that because I have you, I have the spirit of joy! I pray that you will help me to not allow the circumstances of my life to determine my level of joy and happiness. Please prompt me whenever I allow my circumstances to become bigger than you. Help to me live my life to the full, even in the tough circumstances and situations of life. Thank you that I have a life right now. I choose to live my life to the fullest and to enjoy every minute.

DON'T MISS THE MIRACULOUS

TODAY'S SCRIPTURE

"There is a lad here who has five barley loaves and two small fish, but what are they among so many?"

JOHN 6:9

Staying full of God needs to be our greatest priority. One of the easiest ways we can accomplish this is by celebrating small victories in life. This very act keeps us from despising the day of small things.

When we put our attention on the things that have not yet happened, it's so easy to remove our eyes from the things that are happening. While we all love to see the spectacular in our lives, we can so easily miss the miraculous if we are only looking for the spectacular. Yes, it's most often when we learn to celebrate in the simplicity of the small things that have happened in our lives, that the spectacular breakthroughs will begin to take place.

OVERFLOW

When Jesus saw that the crowd was hungry in John 6:5 He said, "Where shall we buy bread, that these may eat?" I love the next verse that says, "But this He said to test them." The disciples were scrambling to come up with a solution. They saw a boy with five barley loaves and two small fish.

They initially despised the small beginning because they were only looking for something spectacular. Jesus loved to celebrate and give thanks for what was in front of Him. Notice that when Jesus took what He had and gave thanks, the bread and fish did not spectacularly appear in a huge pile in front of Him. Rather, the miracle unfolded after He gave thanks for what He had and began to distribute what was in front of Him.

When we begin to celebrate the small breakthroughs in our lives, we won't despise the day of small things. Plus, we will be positioning ourselves to stay full of God and live in the abundance of supernatural supply.

PERSONAL APPLICATION

1. In what areas of my life have I taken my eyes off the good that has happened, regardless of how small the breakthrough?

2. Take five minutes right now and list ten things that you can celebrate in some level of breakthrough.

3. In the Old Testament, the Israelites would assemble stones as a monument to remember what God did for them. Think of ways you can remind yourself of the miraculous that has taken place in your life.

4. Take a moment today to share with a friend about the faithfulness of God in your life.

PRAY THIS TODAY

Father, I thank you that you are the God of abundance. I want to take time right now to thank you for every breakthrough that I have seen in my life, even the smallest breakthroughs of provision. I pray that you will help me to be a person so full of thankfulness that I will never again despise the day of small things. Help me to never miss another miracle because I was only looking for the miraculous in the spectacular. Give me grace to take action to utilize and distribute the small things I do have in front of me. I thank you that you are not the God of just enough, but you are the God of more than enough!

GOD OF THE MOUNTAINTOPS AND VALLEYS

TODAY'S SCRIPTURE

Then the servants of the king of Syria said to him, "Their gods are gods of the hills. Therefore they were stronger than we: but if we fight against them in the plain, surely we will be stronger than they."

1 KINGS 20:23

Both in the healing ministry and in everyday life, we find ourselves having mountaintop experiences. In those moments, God feels so close and it feels like He is fighting on our behalf. But then there are times when we feel like we are in the valley, defeated and beaten down by life. It is critical when we feel like we are in the valley, that we stay full of God by reminding ourselves that God is also the God of the valleys and that He will never stop fighting on our behalf.

In 1 King 20:23 the Syrians made one the greatest errors they could make. The Israelites had defeated the Syrian army in the mountains, so the Syrian advisers suggested that they fight the Israelites on the plains and in the valleys, stating that Israel's God was a God of the high places alone. The Syrians fought them in the valleys, but the Israelites were victorious once again.

So whether you are enjoying a mountaintop experience or you feel like you are in a valley, the good news is that God is not only God of the mountaintop experience; He's also the God of the valley and He's right there with you and fighting on your behalf. This is critical to understand so you can stay full of God. His goodness is not based on your circumstances. Regardless of your circumstances, He is still good and fighting on your behalf.

PERSONAL APPLICATION

1. Where in my life have I based my understanding of the goodness of God only upon the victories and mountaintop experiences of life?

2. How can I better position myself when I am in a valley of life to remind myself that God is still with me, fighting on my behalf?

3. Do I tend to be closer to God in my mountaintop experiences or in the valleys? Why? How could I be close to God regardless of my circumstances?

PRAY THIS TODAY

Father, I thank you that you are always with me and always fighting on my behalf. I thank you that you are the God not only of the mountaintop experiences, but also the God of the valleys and low places. I declare today that I will stay full of You because I will feast on the fact that You are fighting on my behalf. Your goodness is not based upon my circumstances.

A TANK OF GAS OR A BUCKET OF WATER

TODAY'S SCRIPTURE

But you have an anointing from the Holy One.

1 JOHN 2:20

I remember receiving a devastating phone call informing me that the person I had been ministering to had just passed away. The following day, I was driving to speak at a church conference when the students in my car began to ask me about the healing ministry. I discussed with them the tension of seeing incredible breakthrough but at the same time experiencing painful loss, sometimes all in the course of 24 hours.

I told them they could approach this issue one of two ways. First, they could view victories as gas and their losses as a bucket of water on their internal fires. Or they could view not only their victories as gas on their fire, but also view painful losses as even more fuel to their fire. I want my losses to push me closer to God and allow the pain of the loss to fuel my fire. At that moment, a car passed, pulling directly in front of me, when I noticed their license plate read "More Gas."

If we allow our losses to be a bucket of water on our fire, it will be difficult to consistently walk in the abundance of Heaven that God has placed inside us. It's so important that we stay focused on the abundance of Heaven so we can stay full of God during both victories and losses. Let's treat every situation as a bucket of gas to throw on our fires.

A TANK OF GAS OR A BUCKET OF WATER

PERSONAL APPLICATION

1. What circumstances in my life have I allowed to be a bucket of water on my flame?

2. Have I allowed losses to create distance between God and myself or allowed it to push me closer to God?

3. How can I practically apply painful loss in my life to be gas instead of water on my fire?

OVERFLOW

4. Are there things I learned from my losses that can be gas on my fire?

> **PRAY THIS TODAY**
>
> Father, I thank you that you have already placed the abundance of the Kingdom of Heaven inside me. I thank you that I have an anointing from the Holy One that is alive and burning within me. I pray that you will help me to allow both my victories and my losses to be more gas on the fire I already have.

STOP CONDEMNING YOURSELF!

TODAY'S SCRIPTURE

"Woman where are those accusers of yours? Has no one condemned you?" She said, "No one, Lord." And Jesus said to her, "Neither do I condemn you; go and sin no more."

JOHN 8:10-11

I meet so many Christians that are drowning in guilt, condemnation, and sin. Yet when this woman was caught in adultery, Jesus asked her, "Woman where are those accusers of yours? Has no one condemned you?" (John 8:10). Notice that Jesus had the woman declare the answer out of her own mouth, "No one Lord" (John 8:11). Then Jesus said to her, "Neither do I condemn you; go and sin no more" (John 8:11). The power to go and sin no more lies in first recognizing that there is actually no condemnation in Christ. As Christians we are actually in Him and He does not condemn Himself.

Many times we carry guilt for things that we have long been forgiven of. We walk around with condemnation from something we did many years earlier that we have already repented of. If there is no condemnation by God, why do we have the right to condemn ourselves?

When we don't forgive ourselves it leads to depression and sickness. Forgiveness belongs to Jesus and our refusal to forgive ourselves puts us in His place and we end up setting a higher standard than God Himself. We can judge in the sense of evaluating ourselves, but we should not condemn ourselves.

Condemnation does not belong to us. If God has not condemned us, we can't condemn ourselves. If we have walked in condemnation, we need to repent of putting ourselves in the place of God.

We will never stay full of God if we walk in self-condemnation. It's like trying to drive a car with a hole in the gas tank; as fast as the gas goes in, it will flow out. And then we wonder why we are not functioning as God designed us.

Now open your mouth and declare, "No one condemns me, including myself." And then begin to walk in a life of freedom that Jesus paid for.

PERSONAL APPLICATION

1. Do I recognize that Jesus paid for my sin, guilt, shame, sickness, and condemnation?

2. Are there areas in my past from which I still walk in guilt and condemnation?

3. Are there areas in my life where I need to not be so hard on myself?

4. Take a moment and ask Jesus what He thinks about you.

> **PRAY THIS TODAY**
>
> Father, I thank you for your great love for me. At the cross you made Jesus, who knew no sin, to be sin for me so that I could become your righteousness. I thank you Jesus, that you died for my sins once and for all. You died to take all my guilt and all my punishment. You bore my sins once and for all. Likewise, I count myself dead to all guilt, commendation, and punishment of all my sins, because You bore them for me. I thank you, Father, that I am the righteousness of Christ, apart from my works, good or bad. I declare that I will no longer entertain the thought that I may have displeased you. I declare the reality of your Word that says I am the righteousness of God. I am, present tense, the righteousness of God in Christ, completely apart from all my works.

JESUS ON EVERY PAGE

TODAY'S SCRIPTURE

For by Him all things were created that are in heaven and that are on earth, visible and invisible, whether thrones or dominions or principalities or powers. All things were created through Him and for Him.

COLOSSIANS 1:16

One of the things that I find most fulfilling in helping me to stay full of God is recognizing during my Bible reading that Jesus is on every page of the Bible. He is in every circumstance of life and it's our adventure to find and discover Him.

In every day of life, I love to find Jesus within my circumstances. It helps me stay connected to Him and keep Him as the center of my life so I don't lead life by my experiences only. I love the experiences I have, but it is really important to me that Jesus is central.

OVERFLOW

Even when things go wrong and through the tough moments of life, I encourage you to look for Jesus. Look for the good and for what you can learn through the situation.

In your Bible reading, enjoy the discovery of finding Jesus on every page. He appears in the flesh in Matthew, but He's also eternal. From the beginning of the Bible to the end, He's there. You will discover Him in Genesis, as the second Adam. In Exodus, as the stick that touched the bitter water and made it sweet. The stick represents a tree, the tree represents the cross, and when the cross touches something bitter in your life, it turns sweet! You will find Him as the person of Isaac, Abraham, Boaz, Gideon, and Joseph. Scholars say that Joseph is the closest image to the person of Jesus. I found over 40 similarities between Joseph and Jesus.

Jesus is waiting to be discovered. He is not hiding from you, He hiding for you and He's delighted when you discover Him.

PERSONAL APPLICATION

1. How central is Jesus to my daily Christian walk?

2. What biblical character do I want to study to discover their similarities with Jesus?

3. When circumstances in life go wrong, do I stay Jesus-centered?

4. How do I practically keep Jesus at the center of my life?

PRAY THIS TODAY

Jesus, I thank you that all things were created through you and for you. I pray that you will help me discover you in every situation and throughout the pages of the Bible, as well as to keep you central in my life. You are wonderful!

THE GIFT OF RIGHTEOUSNESS

TODAY'S SCRIPTURE

For if by the one man's offense death reigned through the one, much more those who receive abundance of grace and of the gift of righteousness will reign in life through the One, Jesus Christ.
ROMANS 5:17

This has to be one of my favorite verses in the Bible. As a child, when I used to read James 5:16 that says, "The effective, fervent prayer of a righteous man avails much," I used to think that it said, "The effective, fervent prayer of a perfect man avails much."

As a young minister on my journey into discovering God, I learned that righteousness is, in fact, a gift. As a righteous man I could expect to see Heaven shift because of my prayers. I became so thankful because it was no longer my perfection that moved Heaven, it was Christ's perfection.

The way that I reign over circumstances in my life is by understanding that righteousness is a gift. It is not by my perfection, merits, works, or deeds that my prayers get answered. It is because I have received the gift of righteousness. I am righteous and cannot be any more righteous now than the day I was saved!

If you are reading this and thinking that I am advocating living a life that is not pleasing to God, that is not the case. When we truly understand our righteousness (right-standing with God) we will live victoriously over sin and every circumstance of life.

The phrase from Romans 5:17 that says, "those who receive abundance of grace and of the gift of righteousness" shows that righteousness is indeed a gift. And the best way to receive a gift is to say, "Yes, please," and "thank you!"

This is a key verse to staying full of God. It helps us understand that righteousness is a gift and because we have received that gift, we are right with God. We are not working towards righteousness, we are working from His righteousness. We are already righteous.

PERSONAL APPLICATION

1. What performance tendencies do I still operate in regarding righteousness?

2. What can I do to better understand my righteousness, and that, as a believer, I am already right with God?

3. Read the story in Matthew 15:21-23. Ask yourself, why in verse 23 did Jesus answer her "not a word"? You can discover what I found in my book Walking in Supernatural Healing Power.

OVERFLOW

4. If "because as He is, so are we in this world" (1 John 4:17), what is He? Then what does that make you?

PRAY THIS TODAY

Father, I thank you that righteousness is a gift from you and that I cannot earn it by works or merits. I thank you that I am righteous and I cannot become any more righteous than the day I accepted Christ. I pray that you would give me a greater revelation of righteousness, so that I can walk in the freedom that you purchased and can reign in life. Now stand in front of the mirror and declare over yourself out loud, "I am the righteousness of Christ."

ENJOYING THE JOURNEY

TODAY'S SCRIPTURE

I know how to be abased, and I know how to abound. Everywhere and in all things I have learned both to be full and to be hungry, both to abound and to suffer need. I can do all things through Christ who strengthens me.

PHILIPPIANS 4:12-13

It is no surprise to anyone that the journey of life takes us on all sorts of twists and turns up hills and into valleys. There are times of abundance and times of lack, times of hope and times of despair. It is important that we realize we are on a journey and the best thing that we can do is enjoy the process of the adventure of growing in faith. There will be some successes that we will only achieve in life by first experiencing failure, but we can still learn from the experience and enjoy the process of growth.

A friend of mine, who is a very successful business man, told me that he had lost millions of dollars on bad investments. But it's what he said afterwards that rocked me. He said that he never treats it as a loss, but rather as a research and development expense. He grows from the experiences by learning from each "failure." That is what has made him so successful today.

In the same way, on my journey into the miraculous, there have been many times where I didn't see breakthrough. However, I have had to learn to not beat myself up and to enjoy the journey of growing in God. One day I was really beating myself up over a situation and God spoke clearly to my heart and asked me what I was doing. "Punishing myself," I replied. He replied, "My son, Jesus has already taken your punishment, so stop beating and punishing yourself. Start enjoying the process of learning to grow on the journey." That was such a life-giving moment of recognizing that I have permission to go easy on myself and don't have permission to beat or punish myself.

Friends, whatever it is that you are facing today, learn to enjoy the process. Look at it as research and development. Learn contentment simply because you have Jesus.

PERSONAL APPLICATION

1. Have I been punishing myself for certain things?

2. Take a few moments to focus on the cross and the price Jesus paid in full for you.

3. What situations am I currently in that I could look at as research and development and learn from the experience?

OVERFLOW

4. What are lessons that I have learned from failures?

> **PRAY THIS TODAY**
>
> Father, I thank you that I am on a journey of learning to grow with you. I ask that you would help me in the process of enjoying the journey and that you would teach me to be easy on myself. Help me to laugh at myself. I thank you for my research and development fund and that I have a lot of experience and wealth to draw upon. Help me both when I am abased and abounding to be content because I have Christ.

ALL THINGS

TODAY'S SCRIPTURE

And we know that all things work together for good to those who love God, to those who are the called according to His purpose.

ROMANS 8:28

This verse speaks to my heart and fills me with eternal hope. The word "all" means everything. It does not mean half of the issues you have or everything but that one thing you are concerned about. The word "all" means just that: "all."

I was pondering this verse one day in light of our daughter's situation and some particular concerns. I went through the whole verse and reminded myself that "all" means "all." That alone encouraged me. He wants to take care of all of the details in our lives. He cares for all of them and everything that concerns us. So as I was thinking about this particular verse and how it applied to my situation, I got a text from my friend. She had just woken up from a dream and told me that God was going to cause all things to work together for good and that He was taking care of all of the details for me. It was so encouraging!

Whatever concerns you are carrying today, whatever circumstances seem overwhelming, whatever the situation that you're in, regardless of how bad it might look, God can and will work all things together for good. Sometimes in the midst of our situation we aren't able to see how that will be true, but later as we look back we can see God's divine tapestry woven through our lives and how all things worked out for good. Sometimes the best thing we can do is rest, knowing that as we rest God is working on our behalf.

PERSONAL APPLICATION

1. Are there concerns in your life that you don't think God is taking care of for you?

2. Think of a situation from the past that was difficult, but afterwards Jesus worked out for your good.

3. Take a moment to thank God that He is going to work everything together for good in an area that you are currently facing.

4. Choose to meditate on Romans 8:28 throughout the day today and ask God to give you insight into an area of your life that is concerning you.

> **PRAY THIS TODAY**
>
> Thank you, Holy Spirit, that you are concerned about all of our stuff. Thank you that you are working all things together for good, which includes everything that seems hard or impossible, and every situation that requires an "and suddenly" of God. Thank you that you only have good plans for me and I ask that you would help me to remember that you are indeed causing all things to work together for my good. Thanks Jesus.

TAKING TIME TO REST

TODAY'S SCRIPTURE

And after Boaz had eaten and drunk, and his heart was cheerful, he went to lie down at the end of the heap of grain; and she came softly, uncovered his feet, and lay down.

RUTH 3:7

A number of years ago, I was extremely busy doing great things for God. I remember the day and could show you the location where God spoke to my heart. It was the closest to the audible voice of God that I have heard, that said, "You love what you do for me more than you love and enjoy me." We all love doing great things for God and many of us are wired to be doing these things. I myself don't do well sitting around doing nothing.

The story of Ruth is a favorite of mine and part of the story pertains to what God spoke to me. Ruth was a Moabite and Boaz was a Jew. Ruth had lost her husband and was in a destitute state. Her mother-in-law had heard about a rich young man, Boaz. He allowed Ruth to glean among the sheaves to provide for herself and her mother-in-law, Naomi.

Ruth ventured at midnight to find Boaz at her mother-in-law's prompting and found him sleeping. She uncovered his feet and lay down and took time to rest. Boaz awakened with a fright and Ruth introduced herself. Boaz redeemed Ruth in the end by taking her as his wife.

When we take time to sit at the Master's feet, enjoy fellowship with Him, and spend time in worship with Him, we receive everything we need. He delights to take us from destitution to provision.

Whatever you are facing today, take time to recognize your heavenly Boaz, Jesus Christ. Taking time to stop from the busyness of life to be still, is not wasted time. Those can be some of the most beneficial and satisfying times, as you worship and acknowledge Him as the provider of all your needs. In those times, we have the opportunity to humble ourselves as we make Him big and allow Him to pour His refreshing life into us. He is our Kinsman-Redeemer!

PERSONAL APPLICATION

1. Do I take time out of the busyness of life to rest and enjoy Jesus at His feet?

2. How can I act more like a human being, rather than a human doing?

3. Do I recognize that Jesus is my provider and all good things flow from Him? Or am I more concerned with where my provision comes from in the natural?

4. How can I make Jesus bigger in my life? (Note: He can't be made bigger than He already is, but we can change our perspective of how we see Him.)

PRAY THIS TODAY

Father, I thank you that it delights your heart when I take time to rest at your feet. Help me to take times of refreshing in the midst of the busyness of life, where I can exalt you from a place of humility and I can be refreshed. I thank you that your heart for me is provision and that at your feet I can receive all that you have for me.

AN ENCOUNTER WITH THE REDEEMING HEART OF GOD

The next section of this book is dedicated to the wonderful men of God that I had the privilege of meeting while ministering in a U.S. prison.

A NOTE TO THE MEN IN THAT PRISON

I would like to thank each of you for what I received from you. I came thinking I was going to minister to you, but I walked away as a richer person, because of how deeply you touched my heart. It truly was the highlight of my year and I so look forward to when we can meet again. You are a treasure to the heart of God.

The journey into the miraculous is really a journey into the heart of the Father. My one desire is to know Him more and to understand His heart and nature towards humanity. In the spring of 2016, I had the opportunity to minister in one of the largest prisons in the U.S.A. It was during this visit that I had an encounter with the heart of the Father and experienced afresh the redeeming nature of God.

The men in that prison are doing Bethel School of Supernatural Ministry via DVD and I can honestly say they were one of the hungriest churches that I have ever been to anywhere in the world. To see these men burn for Jesus genuinely was so inspiring. They challenged me to a new level. They were not performing to get out on good behavior, as many of them will never see freedom outside the walls of the prison. Many of the men were, in fact, the most free men that I have ever met.

While meeting with a smaller group of the men, I was in the midst of completing this writing project, and so I invited them to participate in writing a section on how they stay full of the abundance of Heaven. I wanted to give them an opportunity to have a voice. I figured that if you have been locked in prison for longer than I have been alive, (one man being in solitary confinement for the first 17 years of his imprisonment) and can still be burning for Jesus, then you have something to write about! Within the week of inviting these men, I had all the following pages, which I was so deeply impacted and encouraged by. I have included these as bonus daily readings and pray that you will have a fresh encounter with the redeeming heart of the Father. He loves to take what the world has written off and turn it into great treasure.

With much love,

Chris Gore

DO NOT WAVER

By *RUDY*

TODAY'S SCRIPTURE

He did not waver at the promise of God through unbelief, but was strengthened in faith, giving glory to God, and being fully convinced that what He had promised He was also able to perform.

ROMANS 4:20-21

Most days I go about encouraging people. I encourage them to stand on God's Word and on promises that have been spoken over their lives, either from another brother or sister, or from the Scriptures, or from the Holy Spirit directly. Sometimes circumstances are difficult and we allow them to dictate our feelings and level of faith.

The Bible says that "faith comes by hearing, and hearing by the word of God" (Romans 10:17). Just recently my friend was going through a tough time and was feeling downtrodden and a bit overwhelmed. So I shared a personal experience with her about my daughter.

Three years ago my daughter got really upset over our father/daughter relationship and quit talking to me. This really hurt me and I took it to the Lord. The Lord highlighted in my spirit that He is turning the hearts of the fathers to daughters, and daughters to their fathers (based on Malachi 4:6). Then someone gave me a word that my ministry would be reconciliation.

So I shared with my friend that even though at the moment it might seem that we are not reconciled (because it's been three years), I still declare and believe those promises. I stand on them because my Papa's Word never comes back void.

About two months passed and I asked my friend to look my daughter up on Facebook, and they became Facebook friends. My friend sent me a letter with a stack of pictures and the word "Enjoy." On my daughter's Facebook page were about ten pictures of her in my arms and also more recent pictures. I felt that my daughter's heart was in her father's arms.

The Word of God always proves true. So next time circumstances or outward appearances don't look so good, stand on God's Word and simply trust Him.

PERSONAL APPLICATION

1. What promises has God given you?

2. Do you declare these promises over your life?

PRAY THIS TODAY

Lord, I'm so grateful for your love. I trust in you. You are my refuge and my fortress. I know the words you've given me are a greater reality than my circumstances. Thank you for showing me how you see me. Jesus, you reign over everything!

TRUST AND OVERCOME

By MICHAEL

TODAY'S SCRIPTURE

I can do all things through Christ who strengthens me.
PHILIPPIANS 4:13

Having already completed twenty-three and a half years of a life sentence, I can look back and see how God has helped me wake up and take the next step. Sometimes God gives us what we need instead of what we want. He uses His Word to build us up in every area of our lives.

Even though I believed I was ready for release from prison a little over seven years ago, God was lining me up to go through the rebuilding process. After receiving my first parole denial, a door was opened for me to go through a college vocational course in Microcomputer Applications. This door would lead to more doors being opened so that I would receive real world experiences.

OVERFLOW

Three years later, I received my parole denial for a second time. I received the denial notice through the mail and it hurt deeply because I wasn't shown the common courtesy of being handed the denial letter in person. I actually thought I would receive parole that time, but it was not meant to be. I was going through a season of being rooted and grounded in the Word of God. I had no job, but had plenty of time to dig deeper in the Word. I was beginning to mature in my faith.

Then God opened a door for me to go to a certain unit where I lived in a faith-based dormitory. I also got a job working with computers and had the opportunity to get educated in more than one area. Living in the faith-based dormitory, I knew in my heart that this was it: I would be granted parole. But, to my dismay, I was given a third parole denial. This was a season of understanding what unconditional love looked like.

God has taken me through three different periods of parole denials, but He has helped me to make Philippians 4:13 real in my everyday life.

PERSONAL APPLICATION

1. How can I stay focused on the One who is above all circumstances?

2. What questions do I need to ask myself in order to keep pushing through the circumstances coming against me?

3. What process can I follow that will help me stay full of God no matter what?

OVERFLOW

4. How can I follow David's example in strengthening myself in the Lord?

DECLARE THIS TODAY

Today I declare that my eyes will stay upon God. My circumstances cannot control my decisions. I declare Philippians 4:13 over my life: "I can do all things through Christ who strengthens me." Today I will worship God like David did. I will call on the name of Jesus and stay full of God.

HEAVEN'S EMBRACE

By *JEFF*

TODAY'S SCRIPTURE

But Paul went down, fell on him, and embracing him said, "Do not trouble yourselves, for his life is in him."

ACTS 20:10

About a year ago I went through a very difficult time. I had carried issues of rejection and co-dependency in my life and ministry and all at once I began to be rejected by several members of my inner circle. It was mostly based on miscommunication and misunderstanding, but it was also a result of me finding greater strength in those relationships than I was in Jesus. When that inner circle began to crumble, so did I.

I thank God that I had learned to press into the Father's heart in times of trouble. It was an intense time. I came to a place where I was all alone with the Lord. It's probably where I should have been all along.

One afternoon, I was walking in an open space at the back of the dormitory where I lived. The dorm is about 40 feet wide, so I was walking back and forth crying out to the Father. I was specifically asking Jesus to be my center. Suddenly, I saw Jesus standing before me right there in the dorm. I fell at His feet and wrapped my arms around His legs. I knew then that He was my cord of three strands. Then He told me to stand up. I stood up and He pulled me into a full embrace. I just began to cry in the natural as Jesus held me tight in His arms. He said, "This is where I want you. I love you so much. I am so proud of you. I believe in you. Don't worry about the others for now. I am working on them. You just stay here in my embrace. This is where you belong. You must live your life from this embrace."

It was a very powerful moment that absolutely changed my life. As I read the verse above where Paul embraced the body of dead young Eutychus, I could clearly hear the Father say, "Remember, there is life in Heaven's embrace." It manifested physically and literally that day with Paul in Troas, but this truth also manifests itself every day across the world as people are drawn to the life that can only be found in Jesus' embrace.

Do you want the strength to overcome and the power to change the world? Get it in Jesus' embrace. And then learn to live life from that place.

PERSONAL APPLICATION

1. Where do I find my strength and stability?

2. How well do I know God's heart towards me?

3. Do I live my life from the position of a beloved son or daughter of the King?

4. What obstacles keep me from living every day in Jesus' embrace?

> **PRAY THIS TODAY**
>
> (This is a prayer from my own prayer journal days after having the vision above.)
>
> Father, show me your heart. This is my goal and my one purpose. Open up my heart to receive all you have for me. Let your anointing rest on me in such power that the world around me cannot go unaffected. I want my presence in a room to totally change the atmosphere for your glory. I want more of you, Daddy! I want to spend my life in your embrace. It is the only place that is home to me. It is the place from which all life flows. What a glorious place to be and what a glorious place to rest. Thanks Daddy, for making it my place.

LIVING LIFE FROM THE OVERFLOW

By *JEFF*

TODAY'S SCRIPTURE

Then He went up into the boat to them, and the wind ceased. And they were greatly amazed in themselves beyond measure, and marveled. For they had not understood about the loaves, because their heart was hardened.

MARK 6:51-52

Right after the feeding of the five thousand, Jesus spent a night of prayer on the mountain while His disciples went out onto the Sea of Galilee in a boat. Earlier that day, Jesus had taken five loaves and two fish, and watched as it multiplied in the hands of His disciples. They fed an estimated 20,000 people (when you include the women and children). Not only that, but twelve baskets of leftovers were collected. It was an absolutely mind-boggling miracle.

But later that night, a storm had come and the disciples were on the sea trying to survive. The wind and the natural world seemed to be against them. Jesus left His mountain and began to walk to them on the water. This alone should have reminded them of who He was, but they were terrified at first, until they realized it was Jesus, and then they were greatly amazed after He got into the boat and the wind ceased.

But it is the phrase "for they had not understand about the loaves" that I want to address (Mark 6:52). What had they not understood? They had lived with Jesus as He had performed miracle after miracle. They had seen that there were no limits to His ability to bring Heaven's reality of power and goodness to real situations they experienced on earth. But apparently, their hearts had been hardened to what Jesus expressed to the world by feeding the multitude.

This wasn't just some cool, show-off miracle that Jesus performed. It was a direct overflow of the love Jesus had for the world. Every miracle ever performed is tied directly to the love in the Father's heart for the people He has created.

As Jesus placed the bread and the fish in the disciples' hands, He was literally creating a connection from the heart of Heaven to the hearts of the disciples – a connection that would flow with the river of life itself. Nothing is impossible in the face of this life-giving flow. No sickness, no need, no chaos, no destruction, no attempt of the devil to steal, kill or destroy can stand before the power of life flowing through that connection.

The disciples received that connection into their hands and were expected to be forever changed by it. And in addition, they were expected to let the river of life overflow into the world around them. Once they were connected

LIVING LIFE FROM THE OVERFLOW

to the true heart of the Father, and His love and goodness toward the world, no storm would ever distract them again.

God wanted them to understand in this miraculous feeding of the multitude that if Jesus took two fish and five pieces of bread and fed 20,000 people, that the leftovers, the overflow, would literally feed the world. How many times could twelve baskets of leftovers be multiplied? How many more people could that feed? And what about the leftovers from the multiplied leftovers? There is simply no end.

This is the lesson: when our lives are truly connected to the heart of Heaven and the river of life flows through us with all the love of Heaven in its stream, the world will be turned upside down by our overflow, our leftovers. We simply have to learn to live our lives from the overflow.

PERSONAL APPLICATION

1. What am I doing to maintain a clear and obstacle-free connection to the heart of the Father?

2. Have I assimilated the Father's heart toward me to a deep enough level so as not to be moved by the trials I might face?

OVERFLOW

3. Who are the people in my world that God wants me to cover with the overflow of His goodness right now?

4. Is my vision for what God wants to do through me big enough?

PRAY THIS TODAY

Father, I want to be filled to overflowing with the love you have for your people. Let me be ever astounded by the love you have for me and those around me. I want to always expect you to manifest that love through your miraculous hand. Let my vision be enlarged and let me see as you see, and love as you love. Let me believe for an overflow of what you give me so that the world around me will be changed by it. Teach me to live my life from the overflow of what you pour into me.

THE PRESENCE OF LIFE

By JEFF

TODAY'S SCRIPTURE

Repent therefore and be converted, that your sins may be blotted out, so that times of refreshing may come from the presence of the Lord.

ACTS 3:19

I have lived now for over 14 years in prison for a crime I did not commit. The horrid darkness of prison coupled with the darkness of depression, disappointment, loss, and inexplicable emotional pain has almost suffocated me. But in the abyss of my own despair I found a glorious truth that catapulted me from the depths of a living hell to the very throne of the living God: There is life in the presence of the Lord!

I am sitting on my bunk in my cell as I write these words. My headphones are filled with beautiful worship, my heart is bursting with the joy of Heaven, my eyes are overflowing with tears of overwhelming gratitude toward my Father. It's the greatest of paradoxes: I am a prisoner, yet I am free. Iron bars and razor wire surround me, yet my feet so desperately want to dance as I look into my Daddy's face this morning.

I have learned to lose myself in the presence of my Father. I close my eyes and I see His face. I watch His eyes look back so filled with love toward me. It's like I can see Him with my whole being. Almost like physically absorbing all of His love and peace and goodness while never taking my eyes off of His beautiful face.

The Word says that refreshing comes from this time I spend with Him, but I don't need to be told in writing. I have experienced it so many times in real life. The word "refreshing"[9] is defined as a "recovery of breath" or "revival" making something alive. That's exactly how it feels when I am face to face with my Father. Things are touched in me that bring calm to chaos, joy to fear, and allow me to breathe in deeply the absolute peace that comes with living life from the perspective of Heaven itself. The lies of the devil that enslaved and suffocated me are replaced with the life that was paid for by Jesus at Calvary.

Do you feel dry today? Do you want more of the overcoming life that Jesus offers? Do you have a burning desire to breathe deeply and freely from the very life of Heaven? Find a place to get alone with the Father. Lose yourself in His presence. It is the very source of life. Your life will never again be the same.

---

[9] "Strongs's #403: anapsuxis - Greek/Hebrew Definitions - Bible Tools." 2010. 18 Jul. 2016

PERSONAL APPLICATION

1. When things get rough, where do I run to find comfort and strength to overcome?

2. Is spending time face-to-face with the Father the number one priority in my life?

3. What am I willing to sacrifice to be able to truly live a life overflowing in God's presence?

OVERFLOW

4. Do I want more?

PRAY THIS TODAY

Father, I want more of you. I want Heaven's freedom in my life. Help me to become lost in your presence. Help me run to your face as the source of life itself. I am anxious to know the depths of your heart. Make me a vessel of your presence that can overflow into the lives of everyone I meet. Let the river flow, Daddy! I am ready to be overwhelmed by You.

MEDITATE

By KELLY

TODAY'S SCRIPTURE

This Book of the Law shall not depart from your mouth, but you shall meditate in it day and night, that you may observe to do according to all that is written in it. For then you will make your way prosperous, and then you will have good success.
JOSHUA 1:8

We are always meditating on something. Meditating can be compared to how a cow eats grass. It chews and chews then regurgitates what it has swallowed and chews some more. Meditating is simply pondering something over and over. It is totally up to us to choose what we meditate on. Many choose to mediate by worrying. This is a futile exercise that only fills us us with negative thoughts, which eventually lead to doubt and discouragement. Worry sickens the hearts and dampens the spirit. However, we could also choose to meditate on God's Word. God's Word strengthens, provides hope, and encourages faith. It always supplies the grace needed to overcome every obstacle in life.

The Bible tells us to guard our hearts with all diligence. This can be hard at times, especially when it seems like everything we see exudes negativity. The news media is a smorgasbord of violence, murder, rape, drugs, and all types of immorality. It wouldn't be hard for me to get depressed if I were to focus on this. However, I realize that the truth of God's Word supercedes the acts of what I see. This is the reason that Matthew 6:33 states that we should seek God and His Kingdom first and everything else will be taken care of.

We don't gain victory by focusing on what the enemy is doing, but by focusing on God and what He is doing. Also, we must realize that believing eventually equates to doing. We do things that are in accordance to what we believe. Imagine what would happen if we truly started to understand and believe that He wants to use us to change the world.

God's promises are eternal and His Word is true. That being said, guess what? I've read the whole story, and in the end, we win!

THE PRESENCE OF LIFE

PERSONAL APPLICATION

1. How would my actions change if I truly believed that God wanted to use me to change the world?

2. What Scripture does God want me to meditate on today?

3. How can I begin exchanging the facts of what I see with the truth of God's Word?

4. Get alone with God and ask Him to give you a word to stand on and begin to meditate on it. Can you begin believing Him for this? How can you claim the promises you don't yet see?

DECLARE THIS TODAY

I believe God's Word. His promises are manifesting in my life. Though I may not see them, by faith I claim them. I am prosperous and I have great success.

GRASSHOPPERS DON'T EAT GRAPES

By KELLY

TODAY'S SCRIPTURE

And the Lord spoke to Moses, saying, "Send men to spy out the land of Canaan, which I am giving to the children of Israel...." And they gave the children of Israel a bad report of the land which they had spied out, saying, "The land through which we have gone as spies is a land that devours its inhabitants, and all the people whom we saw in it are men of great stature. There we saw the giants (the descendants of Anak came from the giants); and we were like grasshoppers in our own sight, and so we were in their sight."
NUMBERS 13:1-2, 32-33

After the children of Israel were delivered from bondage by the mighty hand of God, they still had a problem. They didn't know who they were. Through the eyes of fear, they saw themselves as insignificant grasshoppers in a world full of giants. God wanted to show them the fruit that was to become theirs, a land overflowing with goodness, a land of milk and honey. The fruit that God wanted to give them

OVERFLOW

was an inheritance, a future, and a hope. He was giving them purpose and an amazing destiny.

Sadly, because of their perspective, that generation got a small taste of the fruit, but never owned it as their own possession. There is a big difference between occasionally going down to the local grocery store for a small bag of fruit and actually owning an orchard. Once you own the land, you are then able to get fruit whenever you want.

About six years ago, I took a college-level horticulture class. On one particular day of class, the lesson was about grasshoppers. The instructor explained that grasshoppers would completely destroy fruit vines, such as our grapevines. He expounded that they would consume all of the leaves on the vine, yet, they couldn't eat the fruit itself. Their mandibles are too soft. They can get right up to the delectable, sweet, succulent fruit, but they can't bite into the skin of the grapes. As the grasshoppers consume the energy producing leaves, the vine dies and its fruit rots. Instead of enjoying the fruit that the vine has to offer, they kill all hope of others being able to get the fruit.

Many times God will speak to us, giving us little glimpses of the wonderful things that He has in store for us. He speaks to us through Scripture, prophetic words, circumstances, other people, etc. He will give us new desires in our hearts and show us dreams and visions. Our Father wants us to be aware of the goodness that He planned for us so we will be saturated with hope. Hope is what propels us forward. Hope causes us to desire and passionately pursue the abundance that God has for us. Hope leads us to trust God even when we aren't experiencing that abundance yet.

God will always give you the hope you need to operate from the realm of faith and overcome fear and doubt. Then God will give you authority over that which you have overcome. When you go to battle and win, the land becomes yours as a possession.

PERSONAL APPLICATION

1. In what areas do I feel like a grasshopper? Spend some time alone with God and ask Him how He sees you in those areas.

2. What territory is God desiring me to take for His Kingdom?

3. What testimonies (previous fruit) can I use to remind myself of the wonderful plans God has for me?

4. Are there any grasshoppers in my life that seem to steal my hope? How should I handle them?

DECLARE THIS TODAY

I am not a grasshopper. I am a giant-killer. I am overcoming everything that comes against me, for God says that no weapon formed against me shall prosper. I now own the land that I have overcome and the fruit is mine. My hope is in the Lord and His promises sustain me.

EXPANDED BY LOVE

By CHINO

TODAY'S SCRIPTURE

That Christ may dwell in your hearts through faith; that you, being rooted and grounded in love, may be able to comprehend with all the saints what is the width and length and depth and height—to know the love of Christ which passes knowledge; that you may be filled with all the fullness of God.
EPHESIANS 3:17-19

God will challenge us as believers in order to expand our hearts with His love. Think about it, God is love, through and through. It's His desire to stretch and expand us so we can come to an intimate understanding of that love. God is infinite. There is no end to Him and there are no limitations. If He is that vast, how can we think that a small spiritual foundation would suffice to support all God desires to deposit in us? God knows that we must be stretched and expanded in order to contain greater measures of His heart, love, and person.

I believe He uses our decisions and choices in life to stretch us. I don't believe God is worried about us making mistakes because He tells us that all things work together for our good. Why do all things work together for good? Because He knows that, regardless of what happens, it can be used to accomplish His purposes in our lives. Those elements can be used to challenge and stretch us no matter what, including prison, mental issues, addictions, tragedies, and so forth. They're not from God, but He uses them simply because they bring forth the fruit of experience. We then have the opportunity for the fruit of the Spirit to manifest in our expansion. God loves the process.

PERSONAL APPLICATION

1. What does it look like when God stretches and expands me?

2. Do I love and submit to the process?

3. How has the fruit of the Spirit manifested in my life in the middle of tough circumstances?

OVERFLOW

4. Who does God want to be for me?

> PRAY THIS TODAY
>
> Father, as your son/daughter I say yes to your desires, plans, and goals for my life. Right now, I declare your goodness and invite you to come. Thank you for stretching and expanding me so I can come into an intimate understanding of your love.

WHO CAN CONDEMN YOU?

By THOMAS

TODAY'S SCRIPTURES

There is therefore now no condemnation to those who are in Christ Jesus, who do not walk according to the flesh, but according to the Spirit.
ROMANS 8:1

Who will bring any charge against those whom God has chosen? It is God who justifies.
ROMANS 8:33 (NIV)

Are you worthy of condemnation and punishment for your past transgressions? Are you still living under the fear of judgment from God, as if He is just waiting to send you to hell? It is God Himself who proclaims us innocent. How much simpler can it be? The judge of the universe says you are innocent and justified in His sight because of the blood of His Son.

OVERFLOW

We as men and women need to understand exactly what our identity is in Jesus and who our Father is. We need to shake off and rebuke the condemnation and shame from our sin nature because that is no longer who we are. That person died. The moment we claimed the blood of Christ we were declared a holy believer, a saint, and sin-free! Satan has men and women of the Kingdom so beaten down and scared to walk in their identities as children of the King because people might think they are walking in pride. In Daniel 4, once Nebuchadnezzar recognized God's authority in his life, he became even greater than he was.

We are champions of the Kingdom. We need to begin walking in our identities so our confidence and honor will flow down to the generations coming after us, establishing a legacy that goes well beyond a couple of generations. We are Kingdom heirs; we were made to roar like the Lion of Judah. We have the Spirit of God within us, something the world responds to. We should be the person who walks into a room turning every head, causing others to ask, "Who is that?" because they noticed the shift in the atmosphere. We are victors in Christ, the ones who walk like champions, heads held high because we are the head and not the tail, the lender and not the borrower. We are the King's kids, not arrogant but confident in our identities, rooted in the Father. This is what will draw men and women to God: the peace that comes from an identity in our Father.

We should not walk around as religion dictates, heads hung, as if we have been beaten up and are carrying the weight of the world. Because honestly, who wants to be like a whipped slave with a heavy burden? You are no longer condemned, but justified though the blood of Christ. Religion wants us to focus on the bloody, broken, cross-bearing Jesus. That part of the Gospel is absolutely important because it shows the price Jesus was willing to pay for us, how far God was willing to go, and how much He'd give to get us back. But that's not the end of the story. My Jesus is the one who defeated the cross when He died, went to hell, kicked the devil's butt, took back what didn't belong to him, preached all through hell, beat down death, rose on the third day, ascended to Heaven victorious, and sat at the right hand of the Father!

You are a new creation, innocent, and a Kingdom heir. Begin to believe and walk as one who is no longer condemned, but alive. You cost too much not to live this way!

PERSONAL APPLICATION

1. Why does God declare that those who put their faith in Christ are righteous and acceptable to Him?

2. What does it mean that God Himself justified me? Do I believe it?

3. If I was an enemy king, who would I fear more, a slave in the other king's palace or the king's son or daughter who knew their identity and authority?

DECLARE THIS TODAY

I am a Kingdom heir. I am the head and not the tail, the lender and not the borrower. I am a child of the King of Kings. The King has declared me innocent. I am no longer condemned. I know my identity and will walk in it. I will leave a legacy for the generations coming after me.

IDENTITY SLAP

By RICHARD

TODAY'S SCRIPTURE

"Behold what manner of love the Father has bestowed on us, that we should be called children of God!"

1 JOHN 3:1

Smack! That sickening sound is your God-given identity slapping you back to the reality of who you really are when you are not acting like it. Don't ever forget that even in the worst of situations you are a precious child of the Most High God. The problem comes when we forget to live like it.

"Tom makes me so mad!" His actions may be frustrating and may make you angry, but is it right to act that way? Another person's actions do not excuse us to act out of anger. Our identity should be grounded in the concrete foundation of Christ's goodness. Once we understand the goodness of God and live from that reality, His goodness will be a distinctive quality that carries us through every situation. When we finally embrace that truth, then we will no longer have to fear an identity slap. We will know who we are in God's Kingdom and will act like it. That is, we will act in honor, love, and respect for others. We will display peace, patience, and kindness. In short, we will display the fruits of the spirit mentioned in Galatians 5:22-23.

So when you are bitter, angry, or unforgiving, get ready to be slapped. Your identity, as a child of God, will make itself known to you and the conviction of the Holy Spirit will remind you that you are so much better than the way you are acting.

PERSONAL APPLICATION

1. Do I truly know my identity in Christ's Kingdom? What is it? (Hint: You are loved far more than you will ever know or understand.)

2. When I am confronted with a tense and unbearable situation, do I act out of my identity or something else?

3. Have I ever been slapped by my identity? If yes, did I heed that warning and change my actions? Have those slaps taught me anything valuable?

> **PRAY THIS TODAY**
>
> Father God, I am relying on your supernatural power to remain in the identity and image of Christ no matter what the circumstances. The transformation from a heart of stone to one of flesh only comes from you God, and I thank you for changing mine.
>
> I declare that I will act Christ like because I am good. I am a new creation.

NEVER NEGLECTED

By *MARK*

TODAY'S SCRIPTURE

How shall we escape if we neglect so great a salvation, which at the first began to be spoken by the Lord, and was confirmed to us by those who heard Him.
HEBREWS 2:3

Early in my new birth I was captivated by Hebrews 2:3 and the Lord highlighted the first part to me as only He can do. "How will we escape if we neglect so great a salvation?" As I meditated in the grip of those words, the Holy Spirit told me to replace the word salvation with the word relationship. It would read, "How will we escape if we neglect so great a relationship?"

Wow! I suddenly realized that salvation was all about having a relationship with our heavenly Father. Everything started to shift and fall into place as I knew relationships are about love and God is love. We love because He first loved us, and without love, whatever we attempt is done in vain.

OVERFLOW

When I trust God to help me have a relationship with Him, I can then be faithful with all the other relationships in my life. The Creator of all creation desires to have a relationship with me and through that relationship I have relationships with others. Every day I am encouraged to wake up, knowing that my heavenly Father has provided a way in which I can help Him create expressions of His love and glory with others.

When we don't neglect what He has given us, we co-create with Him. We are never neglected by Him, therefore, we should never want to neglect Him.

PERSONAL APPLICATION

1. How important is having a relationship to living a fruitful life?

2. What is the greatest part of having a relationship?

3. Can I trust the world to teach me about good relationships?

OVERFLOW

4. Has God ever neglected me?

DECLARE THIS TODAY

My heavenly Father, Abba, desires to have a relationship with me that would express His glory through me as I relate to the world around me. I have a good relationship with God and can learn from Him how to have great relationships with others. With each relationship, God has trusted me with another child of His. I am loved by God and therefore I am able to enjoy loving others.

FREEDOM BRINGS STRENGTH

By *NETS*

TODAY'S SCRIPTURE

Now the Lord is the Spirit, and where the Spirit of the Lord is, there is freedom.
2 CORINTHIANS 3:17 (NIV)

When I was set free from the gangster lifestyle and began spending time with God, He removed my fears and a heaviness of sin that was in my heart. He replaced these with a joy of freedom that I had never before experienced. I have never been the same since.

As Christians, one of the keys to remaining free is to stay constantly aware of the Holy Spirit's presence. The Holy Spirit is always present within us. He lives in us and through us, therefore, His presence is always present. However, we must learn to stay "tuned in" to Him and His voice and see what He is doing to remain in Him. It is in His presence that the works of the enemy are destroyed; chains and yokes are broken, and enemy strongholds are torn down. Lies are replaced with truth and darkness is replaced with light. Freedom then naturally leads to joy. That is the reason Psalm 16:11 states, "In Your presence is fullness of joy." I have yet to meet a man or woman that has been set free and didn't rejoice. This joy, in turn, leads to strength. As Nehemiah 8:10 says, "The joy of the Lord is your strength."

So as we make a conscientious choice to turn our heart and affection to God by recognizing His presence in everything we do, we obtain freedom leading to strength.

PERSONAL APPLICATION

1. How can I stay aware of the Holy Spirit's presence?

2. Is there any area of my life where I don't feel free? Spend time alone with God and receive His freedom.

3. Am I able to rejoice in the goodness of God even in the hard times?

OVERFLOW

4. Where does my strength come from? (See Psalm 18:1-3.)

DECLARE THIS TODAY

I am filled with the Spirit of God, therefore, I have freedom to worship, serve, and be everything God created me to be. I have joy that gives me strength to rejoice on the mountaintop and in the valleys, for it is God's strength that keeps me.

IT'S ALL ABOUT RELATIONSHIP

By *PAUL*

TODAY'S SCRIPTURE

And this is eternal life, that they may know you, the only true God, and Jesus Christ whom you have sent.

JOHN 17:3

Our relationship with God is unique. It's unlike any other relationship we can have in this life. Think about it. Our lives are governed by relationships. Every day we experience life through the relationships we have with things or people. We wake up because we have a relationship with our smartphone and its alarm. We have relationships with businesses that are built on our past experiences with them. We have relationships with people, whether they are friends, family, strangers, or coworkers. Generally, the more we know about the person or thing, the better a relationship we have. The more I get to know my friends, the stronger and closer our relationship grows. The more I learn about my smartphone and its different functions, the more beneficial and useful it is to me.

In my relationship with the Father, the more I get to know Him, the closer we become and our relationship gets stronger. The more I know what my Father wants to do, the more I'll pray and the more miracles I'll see. But what separates my relationship with the Father from all others? It's an internal one. All other relationships in life are external, with things or people that are outside of me. God literally lives inside of me! The more I know Him, the more I become like Him and the more He comes alive in me. What He reveals to me about Himself becomes a part of me; I take on that aspect of who He is. I become the revelation of God in the earth.

It's as we grow in our knowledge of Him that we walk in the place of being filled with His Spirit (Ephesians 5:18). If we're not careful, we can subtly go from pursuing Him to pursuing things related to Him. It could be ministry opportunities, church growth, Bible knowledge, a certain reputation, etc. These are all good things, but not Him.

I encourage you to settle in your heart to make knowing God the sole focus of your life. Purpose in your heart to give up anything and everything just to know His heart. As you get to know Him more, you will be filled with His peace and the strength of His nature. You will enter into that place of grace and rest where striving ceases to exist.

The purpose of the cross was to restore us back to relationship with our Father. Jesus died for relationship. He gave everything, His very best, so that we could have eternal life, which is, "that they may know You, the only true God, and Jesus Christ whom You have sent" (John 17:3).

IT'S ALL ABOUT RELATIONSHIP

PERSONAL APPLICATION

1. Was there a time when God revealed a certain aspect of His nature (e.g. Healer, Provider, Peace) and I began to walk in it and demonstrate it to others?

2. What are some practical ways that I can guard my heart and make sure that I am growing in the knowledge of God?

3. How does knowing God more cause me to walk in the overflow? What does that look like in my life?

PRAY THIS TODAY

Father, I want to know you more. I pray that you would continue to reveal your nature to me in greater levels. I want my relationship with you to be the priority in my life. Please teach me how to can grow in our relationship together. Amen.

OUT OF PLACE

By DEWITT

TODAY'S SCRIPTURE

But Jesus said to him, "No one, having put his hand to the plow, and looking back, is fit for the Kingdom of God."
LUKE 9:62

Hatred, lies, deceit, violence, and selfishness with no compassion or remorse was my comfort zone, yet intuitively I felt out of place. Prison intensified these characteristics into an art form, yet I was never content and could never feel like I belonged. I thought I had all the answers, but the answer always evaded me until God provided one.

In July 2012, my granddaughter was two years and eight months old when my daughter posed a question to me. I had been in prison the majority of my daughter's life. She wanted to know if I would also be in prison away from my granddaughter. I love my daughter and granddaughter, but not understanding how to stay out of prison to prove my love was a dilemma. At the same time that question was asked, I had already planned to stab two people who had crossed my path in the wrong way. Already serving a life sentence, a stabbing would guarantee prison forever. Not having the strength to overcome my pride I went to my cell that night and called upon God for the first time in my life. I had never read the Bible. I cried like a baby that night for the first time in over 40 years. God received me like the father in the story of the prodigal son. I later ended up in the same dorm with the two people I wanted to hurt and testified to them both about the love of Jesus and forgiveness.

Four years later, I've completely read the Bible six times, led a Bible study in a faith-based dorm, and went through an Emmaus Walk and Kairos Weekend. I am one of the facilitators in the School of Supernatural Ministry under Bethel Church in Redding, California.

Do I still get out of place? Of course, but now I know how to stand on the words of Jesus in Luke 9:62 which says, "No one, having put his hand to the plow, and looking back, is fit for the kingdom of God."

PERSONAL APPLICATION

1. How do I know when I am out of place?

2. What do I do to return to God's glory?

3. How do I feel His Spirit of peace and love when I return to Him?

> **PRAY THIS TODAY**
>
> God, I thank you for convicting me when I'm out of place and receiving me with love upon my return to You.

Chris and Liz are New Zealanders that have resided in Redding, CA as apart of Bethel Church for the past 10 years. One of their greatest passions is to see people set free from sickness and disease and to see the body of Christ fully equipped to get Jesus what He paid for. Their surpassing passion is to see believers walk in the daily abundance of Heaven. This new book, Overflow, A Daily Experience of Heaven's Abundance, includes over 30 daily readings full of practical & Scriptural insights to encourage & challenge you to a deeper walk into the abundance of Heaven. Each reading ends with several questions to ponder and a prayer or declaration for personal application. As a bonus, Overflow contains daily readings by prisoners from a maximum security prison in the US. While Chris was ministering in their prison, he encountered the love of the Father and the redeeming heart of God in greater measures. He asked the men to write how they walk in the abundance of Heaven despite being incarcerated, many of them for life sentences. Be prepared for your mind to be transformed as you read this book!

Follow Chris on Facebook:
www.facebook.com/Chrissgore

OTHER BOOK TITLES BY CHRIS GORE

Walking in Supernatural Healing Power
Practical Guide to Walking in Power